# Blender Game Engine Beginner's Guide

THE UNIVERSITY OF
WINCHESTER

Martial Rose Library
Tel: 01962 827306

The non progr

Victor Kuller Ba

PUBLISHIN

To be returned on or before the day marked above, subject to recall.

BIRMINGHAM - MUI

# Blender Game Engine Beginner's Guide

Copyright © 2012 Packt Publishing

First published: September 2012

Production Reference: 2180912

Published by Packt Publishing Ltd.
Livery Place
35 Livery Street
Birmingham B3 2PB, UK.

ISBN 978-1-84951-702-7

www.packtpub.com

Cover Image by Asher Wishkerman (a.wishkerman@mpic.de)

# Credits

**Author**
Victor Kuller Bacone

**Reviewers**
Pang Lih-Hern
Michelangelo Manrique

**Acquisition Editor**
Robin de Jongh

**Lead Technical Editor**
Hithesh Uchil

**Technical Editors**
Rati Pillai
Lubna Shaikh

**Copy Editors**
Brandt D'mello
Insiya Morbiwala
Alfida Paiva

**Project Coordinator**
Sai Gamare

**Proofreader**
Joel T. Johnson

**Indexer**
Rekha Nair

**Production Coordinator**
Melwyn D'sa

**Cover Work**
Melwyn D'sa

# About the Author

**Victor Kuller Bacone** is the pen name for a Blender enthusiast of six years. By profession, he is a video editor, but the explosion of current technologies has led him to learn 3D software, and he chose Blender out of them all.

In the short span of his career within the Blender community in Catalonia (Spain), Victor has promoted Blender events, master classes, and an online magazine under the name **Blendercat** (http://www.blendercat.org) for anyone who wants to learn 3D using free software. His great admiration for the animation and interactive side of Blender is combined with his passion for games, and more specifically, the ease with which one can create games using Blender. He holds a Masters degree in Computer Science, and teaches both young and unemployed adults.

I would like to thank Sisizik, without whose help I couldn't have transcribed this book.

# About the Reviewers

**Pang Lih-Hern** is a Computer Game Engine Programmer with more than five years of industry experience. He started programming when he was 12, learning the quick, basic language. After graduating with a degree in Software Engineering and Games Design from Multimedia University Malaysia, he began his freelancing endeavors, which eventually led him to be a part of the core technical team for John Galt Games (Malaysia). He was a part of the decision-making group for designing and implementing the company's proprietary game engine. Lih-Hern is also actively involved on the open source front, often submitting fixtures and features for the popular, open source Ogre3D engine. One notable contribution of his was the Parallel Split Shadow Map feature that enhances the shadow rendering of a 3D scene. He is also a strong advocate of Blender and is currently holding the position of maintaining the Blender exporter to Ogre3D's mesh format.

After leaving John Galt Games (Malaysia), Lih-Hern co-founded Liquid Rock Games Sdn. Bhd. (outsource development) and Nakama Studios Sdn. Bhd.(in-house development) with his fellow artist partner Yap Chun Fei. The goal was to create innovative, AAA-quality games, without the need for a huge budget cost, by means of using open source technology and tools, such as Blender, Gimp, and Ogre3D. As of now, Nakama Studios (their in-house development studio) is in the process of developing its first, racing title named TrackVerse (formally known as Aftershock), an online, multiplayer, racing construction kit game. The game's artwork have been modeled and textured using Blender and Gimp, showcasing the capability of such tools in the commercial market.

Lih-Hern has also reviewed another book for Blender published by Packt Publishing called *Blender 2.49 Scripting* by *Micheal Anders*.

> First of all, I would like to thank Packt Publishing for giving me the opportunity to review this book. I would also like to thank my family and the co-partner of my company, for allowing me the spare time and support to review this book. This book serves as a nice introduction to the world of game development, to enthusiasts with little or no knowledge in game development. I hope this book will help pave the initial, stepping stones for using the Blender Game Engine to create their own dream games.

**Michelangelo Manrique**, born on May 20th, 1980, has always been interested in Fine Arts. This interest made him not only start his university studies in the History of Art, but also to work as a painter and art curator. Michelangelo also has a love of technology, and he discovered the use of Blender in 2004. Blender caught his attention and he was fascinated by this 3D suite's possibilities and workflow.

He is currently a member of bf-docboard-es, helping with the official wiki translation of the Blender software to the Latin-Spanish community.

Presently, Michelangelo is working as a programmer. He publishes tutorials and writes articles, and at the same time offers different courses for Blender learning. He is available to do freelance or collaborative work with other studios, or for discussion events about the software. Michelangelo is a Blender Foundation Certified Trainer.

For further information, visit `http://www.lighthouseanimation.es`.

Michelangelo has also been working on different areas of software engineering, such as developing websites, managing databases, or programming for `http://www.gpvwc.com`. He is currently working as a full-time programmer at `gamereactor.es`, and is actively involved in the Blender community through publishing articles and offering courses for Blender learning, especially regarding rigging and modeling.

# www.PacktPub.com

## Support files, eBooks, discount offers and more

You might want to visit www.PacktPub.com for support files and downloads related to your book.

Did you know that Packt offers eBook versions of every book published, with PDF and ePub files available? You can upgrade to the eBook version at www.PacktPub.com and as a print book customer, you are entitled to a discount on the eBook copy. Get in touch with us at service@packtpub.com for more details.

At www.PacktPub.com, you can also read a collection of free technical articles, sign up for a range of free newsletters and receive exclusive discounts and offers on Packt books and eBooks.

http://PacktLib.PacktPub.com

Do you need instant solutions to your IT questions? PacktLib is Packt's online digital book library. Here, you can access, read and search across Packt's entire library of books.

## Why Subscribe?

- Fully searchable across every book published by Packt
- Copy and paste, print and bookmark content
- On demand and accessible via web browser

## Free Access for Packt account holders

If you have an account with Packt at www.PacktPub.com, you can use this to access PacktLib today and view nine entirely free books. Simply use your login credentials for immediate access.

# Table of Contents

# Preface

In this book, you will find the necessary tools for the friendly Blender Game Engine. When I set out to write a book for beginners, I was preparing the text of a game called "Save the Whale." Of course, much of the introduction to this text could be applied to the first chapters of the book you have in your hand. So mostly, some of the exercises you will find are extracted from a game idea of mine, which eventually helped me explain many of the concepts of Blender Game Engine, such as how Blender's interface works, and what kind of connections must be learned to move our character within our own game.

BGE is a section of the Blender program that is a free, 3D software package. Blender is very powerful and very complex at the same time. The Beginner's Guide is a gentle introduction, not only for someone interested in learning about games made in Blender, but also for anyone who is curious to know all about what can be done with Blender.

Blender, as you know, is an open source program and has many followers. So much so that the program is complex, involving many fields of work, and you can use it in different disciplines. Parts of the program may be unknown to you if you do not apply them to your project. So a part of the BGE is for beginners, not for those who have not used Blender in their life, but for those who use Blender daily and have not played with the game engine program. This is a powerful tool whose potential you will see in the following pages of this book. Here is a list of the chapters with their brief overview.

## What this book covers

*Chapter 1*, *Things You Need to Know*, starts off with a general overview of what the Blender interface looks like, how to focus in BGE mode, what the Logic Editor is and how it runs. The Logic Editor is simple to use, as determined by using the keys and the actions, which are associated with each object in the scene. A simple explanation of how they connect the bricks will open a world of possibilities.

*Chapter 2*, *Your Characters*, directly starts with BGE, but needs some models for it to work. If we start working with the BGE, then we must have a library of all of the objects we use in our game. On the Internet, we can find plenty of 3D objects that can be useful for our game. We suggest that you use some pages from the best library, and some good advice to create your game.

*Chapter 3*, *The First Level*, begins with the specific objects that we need, with a quick overview of the game level by creating an environment. We will show you how to create the beginning of a game, which marks the start and end of the level of play we created.

*Chapter 4*, *Collisions*, explains some of the most common responses of collisions. This is because collisions are the most important part of our character's interaction with its own universe. This confrontation between the character and everything around it can be very important in the game.

*Chapter 5*, *Gameplay*, explains the next level of the game. It explains how to keep score, the level of life bar, and many more essential constants in the game, regardless of the level of play you are in. In this chapter, we will discuss the most essential topics, such as life bar, counters, maps, or viewpoints.

*Chapter 6*, *Liven Up Your World!*, makes it extremely important for us to improve our game, by animating it and creating the difference.

*Chapter 7*, *Game Menu Screens*, covers the menu screens of a game, and shows how to create menus to start playing, create titles and buttons, and how to create the executable to start the game.

*Chapter 8*, *Publishing Your Game*, creates a first draft, which is playable at the first level of your game that was made in Blender. When you have finished the game or demo, it is time to publicize your game in order to get people to download it and mark their comments. In this section, we show some interesting ideas for the same.

# What you need for this book

This book will not make your game the best, but will only show the fundamental principles of the game engine and how it works with the logic bricks.

For good and best use, I highly recommend the reader of this book to write down his idea of the game on a paper, decide on the character or characters that will be a part of it, the enemies of the characters, and especially how the game environment should look.

A good plan like this will get half the work done. The basic equipment that the user may need later is the Blender program which can be downloaded for free from its official website: http://www.blender.org.

Remember, idea, pen and paper, and then Blender. Do not even begin to reverse this, else you might have too many headaches.

Blender has very low hardware requirements; for more details visit `http://en.wikipedia.org/wiki/Blender_(software)` and `http://wiki.blender.org/index.php/Doc:2.6/Manual/Introduction/Installing_Blender`.

# Who this book is for

If you have used Blender before, but never got a grip of the BGE, then this book is for you. If you have tried and failed with other game development environments, or if scripting is not your strong point, then this is where you should start.

# Conventions

In this book, you will find several headings which appear frequently.

To give clear instructions of how to complete a procedure or task, we use:

## Time for action – heading

1. Action 1
2. Action 2
3. Action 3

Instructions often need some extra explanation so that they make sense, so they are followed with:

## What just happened?

This heading explains the working of tasks or instructions that you have just completed.

You will also find some other learning aids in the book, including:

## Pop quiz – heading

These are short multiple-choice questions intended to help you test your own understanding.

## Have a go hero – heading

These practical challenges and give you ideas for experimenting with what you have learned.

You will also find a number of styles of text that distinguish between different kinds of information. Here are some examples of these styles, and an explanation of their meaning.

Code words in text are shown as follows: "At the bottom of the page, you will find the `file.blend` downloadable."

**New terms** and **important words** are shown in bold. Words that you see on the screen, in menus or dialog boxes for example, appear in the text like this: "We can change the default view and choose the **Game Logic** view..".

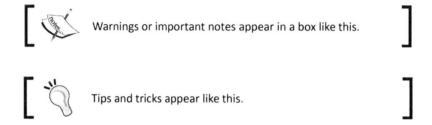

Warnings or important notes appear in a box like this.

Tips and tricks appear like this.

# Reader feedback

Feedback from our readers is always welcome. Let us know what you think about this book—what you liked or may have disliked. Reader feedback is important for us to develop titles that you really get the most out of.

To send us general feedback, simply send an e-mail to `feedback@packtpub.com`, and mention the book title through the subject of your message.

If there is a topic that you have expertise in and you are interested in either writing or contributing to a book, see our author guide on `www.packtpub.com/authors`.

# Customer support

Now that you are the proud owner of a Packt book, we have a number of things to help you to get the most from your purchase.

# Downloading the example code

You can download the example code files for all Packt books you have purchased from your account at http://www.packtpub.com. If you purchased this book elsewhere, you can visit http://www.packtpub.com/support and register to have the files e-mailed directly to you.

# Downloading the color images of this book

We also provide you a PDF file that has color images of the screenshots used in this book. The color images will help you better understand the changes in the output. You can download this file from http://www.packtpub.com/sites/default/files/downloads/7027OS_graphics.pdf.

# Errata

Although we have taken every care to ensure the accuracy of our content, mistakes do happen. If you find a mistake in one of our books—maybe a mistake in the text or the code—we would be grateful if you would report this to us. By doing so, you can save other readers from frustration and help us improve subsequent versions of this book. If you find any errata, please report them by visiting http://www.packtpub.com/support, selecting your book, clicking on the **errata submission form** link, and entering the details of your errata. Once your errata are verified, your submission will be accepted and the errata will be uploaded to our website, or added to any list of existing errata, under the Errata section of that title.

# Piracy

Piracy of copyright material on the Internet is an ongoing problem across all media. At Packt, we take the protection of our copyright and licenses very seriously. If you come across any illegal copies of our works, in any form, on the Internet, please provide us with the location address or website name immediately so that we can pursue a remedy.

Please contact us at copyright@packtpub.com with a link to the suspected pirated material.

We appreciate your help in protecting our authors, and our ability to bring you valuable content.

# Questions

You can contact us at questions@packtpub.com if you are having a problem with any aspect of the book, and we will do our best to address it.

# 1
# Things You Need to Know

*The **Blender Game Engine** (**BGE**) is one of the most interesting parts of Blender. This book will help you to get started and make games by modeling low poly objects and animated interactive characters, and use them in the Game Engine with basic controls and more. To learn the BGE, you'll need to learn a Node Editor which provides you with an easy-to-use visual interface (logic blocks) to design games without requiring any knowledge of programming.*

The Node Editor has a visual way to set up Composite and show the results. Logic blocks can be connected, which together allows you to create visually complex results. There are three different types of logic blocks in the BGE: sensors, controllers, and actuators. Each of these has a different number of sub-types. Using this system, you can make a character respond to your keyboard input events or set up some basic **Artificial Intelligence (AI)** behavior for your enemy characters, objects, or environments of the game.

To make games with Blender, we can begin in the section called Logic Editor (sections in Blender are called editor types). Game Logic is what causes anything to happen in the game. The blocks (or "bricks") that you can see represent pre-programmed functions that can be tweaked and combined to move the player, interact with the world, change the level, and more. In short, it helps you create the game.

At the beginning, we do not need cool models, only a cube (by default, Blender shows it) to represent our player in order to move in our 3D environment. We will learn how to move it and how it collides with a wall (**plane**). If we do that, we can then proceed to substitute our poor model (a cube) and wall for a cool character and good environments. Are you ready?

This book assumes that you haven't had any, or very little, experience in using Blender, so we will go through these chapters step-by-step.

In this chapter we shall:

◆ Find out about the Interface of the **Logic Editor**

◆ Learn how to use the **Logic Bricks Editor**

◆ Start the **Game Engine**

# Things you need, and things you don't

The basic equipment that you need to make a Blender game is the Blender program, which you can download for free from its official page at www.blender.org. It would be better to use the latest version, but it is not necessary. You can make an executable game and then others could play your game without needing to install Blender. Blender runs in most of the common operating systems such as Windows, Linux, and Mac. If you have a standard computer, you have the basic requirements to install a copy of Blender.

If you have never used Blender before, I would recommend you to spend a bit of time reading the documentation and try to do some tutorials provided on Blender's website. You might also find it useful to spend time reading some of Blender's beginner tutorials on other websites. This will help you learn techniques of Blender that we don't show in this book. These friendly websites will answer some of the basic questions that you might have about how to use Blender in modeling, texturing, animation, and others that we do not cover completely.

Surprisingly, all of the information provided on these websites is necessary, but not at this moment, not for your first Blender experience. Creating a lot of (Blender) games will surely help improve your knowledge. Blender uses a visual click-and-drag system to create basic game interactions. This allows the BGE to be used by everybody, including those who may not be programmers. Blender also has a programming language, Python, which can be used to create more complex game interactions. For the purposes of this book, we will focus on the visual system for creating games only. When you have learned the basics of using the BGE, you can then follow more advanced tutorials which show you how to implement Python scripting to create more complex games.

As you may know, Python is a programming language. Python can be used as an extension language for existing modules and applications that need a programmable interface. It has the design of a small language with a large standard library and an easily extensible interpreter. Most Python implementations can function as a command-line interpreter, for which the user enters statements sequentially and receives the results immediately.

Python is essential to make better presentations with the characters, animations, and the rest of the game, but it is not necessary that you use it. Someone can help you in the parts where you do not know enough. The only thing you need to know is how you use logic bricks. Later, you will improve on the rest. Blender's popularity and faithful following has been growing rapidly since its first release in 1998. This has led to a large number of individually-run websites focused on Blender. Go to the official Blender site to see a selection of the websites dedicated towards helping the community.

# Time for action – start using the BGE

Let us start and open the Blender program. Closing the splash screen then reveals Blender's default scene that is composed of a main view surrounded by other panels. The main area in the center of the screen is the **3D View,** as shown in the following screenshot. By default, this contains a **cube** as I had mentioned earlier in the chapter.

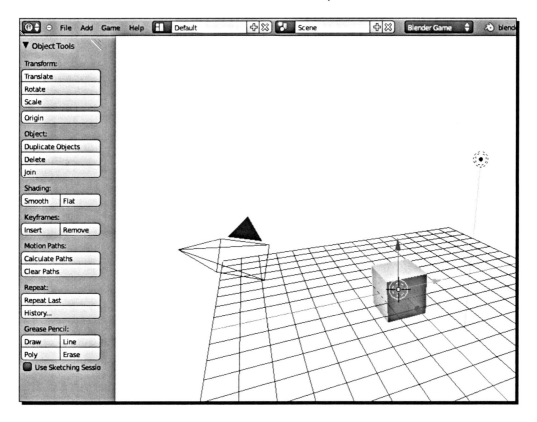

We can change the default view and choose the **Game Logic** view. To do this, go to the top menu bar and click on the icon next to **Default**. The drop-down menu will show several preset views, as shown in the next screenshot. We can choose the one that interests us, which right now, is the **Game Logic** view.

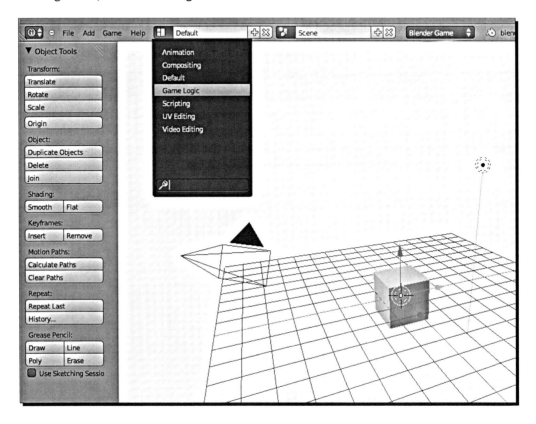

## What just happened?

Blender's flexibility with windows lets you create screen layouts for different tasks, such as **Animation**, **Compositing**, **Default**, **Game Logic**, **Scripting**, **UV Editing** and **Video Editing**. It is often useful to be able to quickly switch between different environments within the same file. For each task, you need to set the stage. In this example, we selected the **Game Logic** view for our main purpose of making games.

Use the window controls to move frame borders. When you have a layout that you like, and wish to use it as your favorite layout, click on the **+** button to save the layout as a new preset layout template. Obviously, if you want to delete it, click on the **X** button.

# Exploring the interface of the Logic Editor

Alas! There are so many panels and everything seems so confusing. Do not worry, my first impression was the same. However, by the end of this chapter, you will be familiar with most of the on screen elements. When you create a game with Blender, you do not work with only one editor type. But without **Logic Editor**, it is not possible to make a game.

Knowing the interface of the **Game Logic** view offers insight into how the Logic Editor works and prepares us to make complex connections in our game truly interactive.

**The Game Logic** layout is divided into areas by default, each of which has a particular function or purpose, depending on what the user is doing at that time. There are **Header** areas in each display editor type. Using these headers (pointed out by the arrows in the next screenshot) we can swap between different editor views. We will focus on the bottom display called **Logic Editor** (bottom left header).

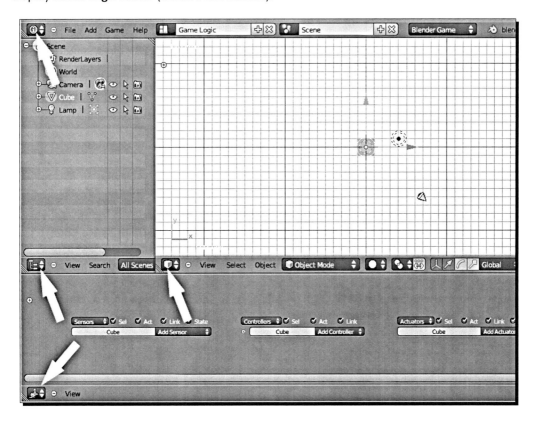

If you want to zoom in/out of the Logic Editor work area, you must press *MMB* (middle mouse button) and move it. If you want to pan work areas click *Shift* button + *MMB*. Choose *Ctrl* button if you have Mac OS

The Blender Game Engine uses logic bricks (a combination of sensors, controllers, and actuators) to control the movement and display of objects in the engine.

◆ **Sensors** sense events, for example, a key press or mouse movement. Sensors are linked to controllers which compare them.

◆ **Controllers** check (true or false) and combine these pulses to trigger the proper response and activate the last group: actuators. They can also be thought of as conditional rules.

◆ **Actuators** initiate their functions when they get a positive pulse from one (or more) of their controllers.

We will explain shortly these three parts of logic bricks and set up a very basic system within the game panel by showing how to use a sensor, controller, and actuator.

 The list menu of an object's logic is only visible when the object(s) are active (shown in white in the outliner panel). Be sure the cube is selected (if not, click on it in the 3D View with the right mouse button).

## Time for action – exploring the logic bricks world

All objects have two options, one of which is a label with their name (in this case **Cube**), and the other a button labeled **Add Sensor**. The **Add Sensor** button adds a new sensor to the object. The following steps will help you in exploring the world of logic bricks:

*1.* Select the **Cube** with *RMB*. Click on **Add Sensor** and select **Keyboard** as the sensor in the sub-menu listed:

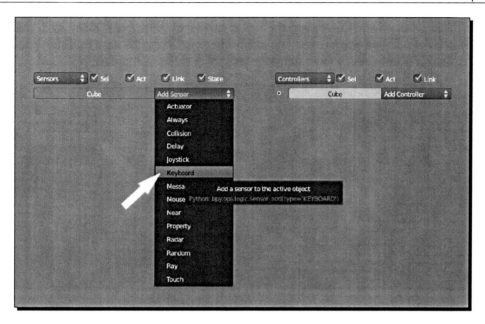

**2.** Be sure to select the cube with *RMB* to operate with logic bricks. Press the *D* key or *Right arrow key* in the blank cell with no label if you want to move the object, for example, to the right. The key that you press will be assigned to the sensor. This is the active key, which will trigger the positive pulse. Click inside the button again if you want to change or un-assign the key:

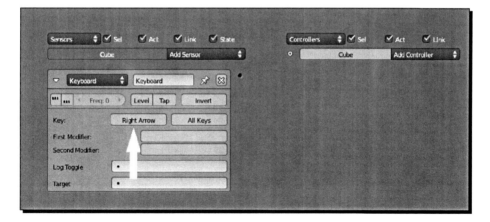

3.  Next, click on **Add Controller**. The first controller in the menu is called **And**. This is the default type when you create a new controller. It can be used to simply pass a **Sensor** event directly to an **Actuator** (as shown in the next point):

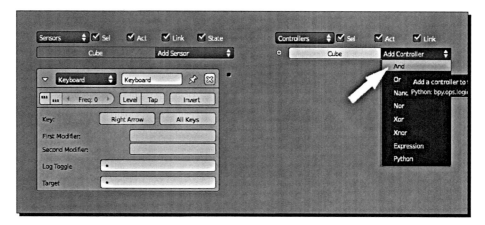

4.  Next, click on **Add Actuators**, and choose **Motion**:

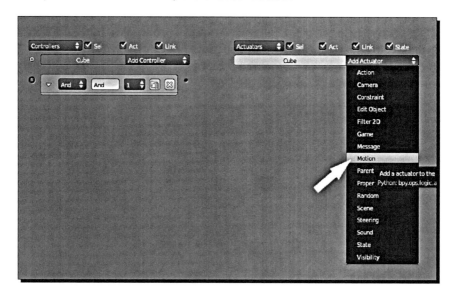

5.  Now, change the value of x axis to 0.20 in **Loc** (Location). The three grey boxes in each row is the motion on the x, y, and z axes (in that order). If you want a diagonal motion, add values to all of the axes at the same time. If you want to rotate the cube, enter 0.20 in **Rot** (Rotation) of x axis:

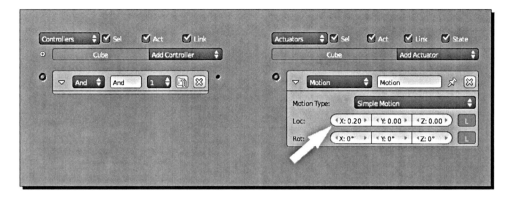

The cube jumps the number of blender units that we input, this can cause objects to go through and around our scene.

The **L** button switches whether the motion will be added to the local or global axis. Local axis is the object's own axis. This is the most common option and is the default. With the global axis, the cube movement can be aligned with the axis of the world.

**6.** We will now connect this blocks system together. Click-and-drag from the socket (small circle) at the end of **Sensor** to the socket at the start of **Controller**:

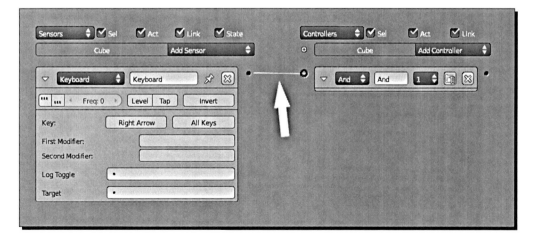

**7.** Then click-and-drag from the socket at the end of **Controller** to the socket at the start of **Actuator**:

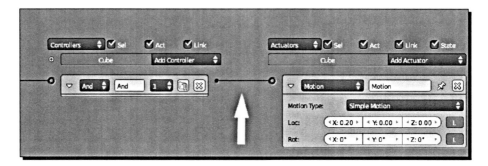

In this example, the sensor is responsible for moving the cube forward if we push the *Right arrow key*.

**8.** Press the **Start** button to play the game in the **Properties Scene** panel:

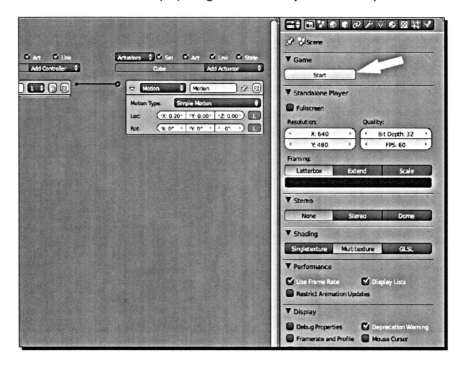

The cube will not move automatically. Press the *Right arrow key*, and it will start to move forwards. When you stop pressing the key, the cube will stop moving. Keep the key pressed to move the cube further. Press *Esc* to return to Logic Editor of Blender.

If you're happy with what you've seen, click on the **Start** button again, you can do it as often as you like.

Change the size of the view in the desired panel by moving the cursor near the limits of the header menus, moving horizontally and then vertically.

You can also press the *Ctrl + Up arrow key* to get a completely maximized view (be sure you click on the **3D View** panel before doing so).

## What just happened?

Great! You just accomplished the three parts of logic bricks, and there is a connection among them. Let's review how to do that and we will be ready to understand the parts!

◆ **Sensor**

The **Keyboard** sensor is for detecting keyboard input. The first blank cell is for single key presses. We pressed the *D* Key, or the *Right arrow key*, to move in the x axis of our cube. Sensors are grouped by objects, with every selected object appearing in a list and under each object are its sensors. It is possible to filter them if we check/uncheck which sensors are viewed. We can select which sensors to be viewed from the following options:

  ❏ **Sel**: Shows all of the selected objects' sensors

  ❏ **Act**: Shows only the active objects' sensors

  ❏ **Link**: Shows the sensors which have a link to a controller

  ❏ **State**: Shows only those sensors connected to a controller of the current state

But for the moment, let us leave them as they are.

◆ **Controller**

The controllers are the bricks that collect data sent by the sensors.

◆ **Actuator**

The actuators initiate their functions when they get a positive pulse from one (or more) of their controllers. They set an object into motion, for example, rotation.

**Simple Motion** applies motions in our cube without frictions. If we need a character with resistance, we need to choose **Servo Control**, which consists of a servo controller that adjusts the force on the object in order to achieve a given speed, and hence the name **Servo Control**. For the moment, **Simple Motion** is right.

Of course, the cube has got only one interactive key, and will go ahead if we push the *Right arrow key* in the keyboard. However, this just introduces us to the fundamentals of the Blender Game Engine. You just need to try, test, and modify it. It is easy, isn't it?

Hey! We are finally programming video games! In some aspects, this is similar to being a computer programmer.

By adding more logic, we are ready to continue making a game. But first, let us try to finish an entire movement of our cube so that you can move freely in our private 3D scene.

## Time for action – moving the cube

To add more movement to the cube, perform the following steps:

1. Press the *Ctrl + Up arrow key* to work with the maximized area of the **Logic Editor** panel. We will be using three more keyboard sensors, let's start creating them.

2. We have a *D* or *Right arrow key* connected. Let's do the rest. Add a new sensor called **Keyboard** again and press the *Left arrow key* in the blank cell as shown in the following screenshot:

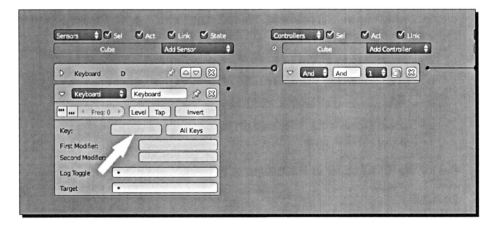

3. Add a new **Keyboard** sensor again and press the *Up arrow key* as shown in the following screenshot:

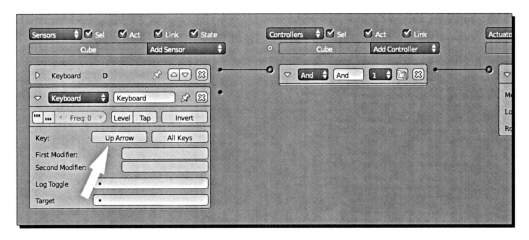

4. For the last one of the keyboard sensors, press the *Down arrow key* as shown in the following screenshot:

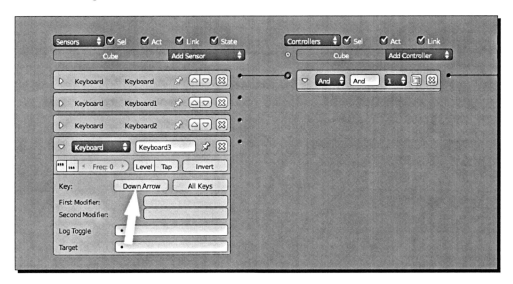

As seen in the previous screenshots, sensors have been closed by clicking on the triangle on the left-hand side of the header to get more space. But we realize that **Keyboard1**, **Keyboard2**, and so on do not mean much to us. I recommend renaming **Sensors** in order to make them accessible and readable in an easy way when we have more sensors in the list.

**5.** Just click on the field that displays, for example, **Keyboard3,** and rename it to Key Down. Use this process to rename the rest of the **Sensors**:

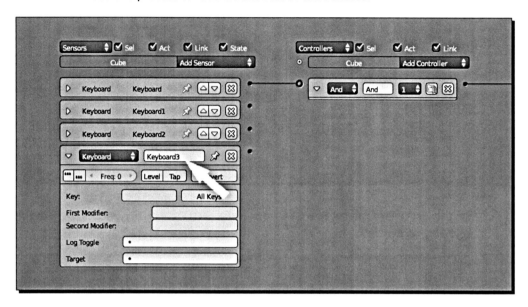

**6.** Add all of the **Keyboard** sensors to a controller each, as we did for the first one, by clicking on **Add Controller**, and select **And** as the controller and connect them each, one to one:

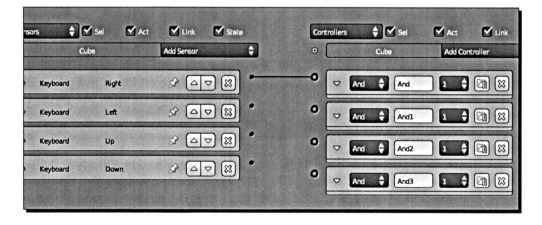

**7.** Add three more **Actuators** by clicking on **Add Actuator** and selecting **Motion**.

Change the value in each cell as shown in the next screenshot. In this case, the left key is assigned -0.20 in x axis and the up/down keys are used for the rotation of our cube, the value of the up key is 0.20 in the **Rot Z** axis and -0.20 for the down key in **Rot Z**.

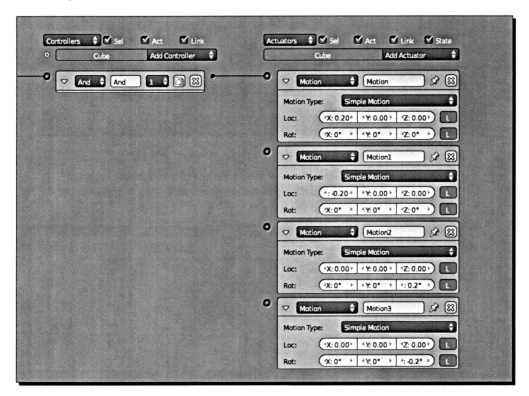

 Of course, we need to rename all our active **Actuators**, similar to how we had renamed our **Sensors** (as shown in Step 5). Spend a little time renaming them to, for example: Move Right, Move Left; Rotate Right and Rotate Left.

At the end of this exercise, our cube should move while we press the key correctly. But wait! The last step is to connect all of the bricks together.

8. Drag-and-drop to connect all of them (as shown in the following screenshot) and just press the *Ctrl + Up arrow key* (minimize the Logic Editor area) and finally press the **Start** button:

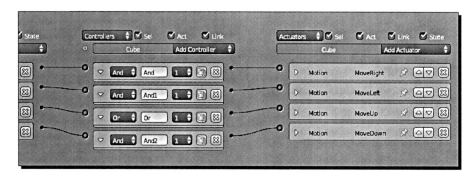

If you wish to maximize the **3D View** area, press the *Ctrl + Up arrow key* after having clicked on the **3D View** area with the *Left mouse button* as shown in the following screenshot:

9. For starting the Game Engine, press *P*. You will be able to move your cube around as shown in the following screenshot:

We can move our cube around the screen. That's fantastic!

## *What just happened?*

We managed to easily and intuitively work with Logic Editor. We created an interaction with our character by adding the following:

◆ Sensors to recognize the keyboard

◆ Basic controllers to link the actuators to the sensors

◆ Actuators that will move the cube, by following the inputs from the keyboard added as sensors

As you have seen, many operations with logic bricks are repeated. But in the end, we change a numeric value of the actuator, which facilitates the learning by repetition so that it's not difficult to understand how the other bricks work.

We learned how to move our cube in the 3D scene by connecting logic bricks. It is as easy as giving orders by using the keyboard. You could increase the mobility options if you have more buttons to press.

## Pop Quiz – exploring the interface of the Logic Editor

1. If you want to create a jump motion, which local axis must you change?

    a. x

    b. y

    c. z

2. Which option do you choose if you want to go in the opposite direction of the x axis while rolling?

    a. Subtract the X value

    b. Add a value less than X

    c. Change the Y value

3. Which cell modifies the values of rotation?

    a. Loc X, Y, Z

    b. Loc in X or Y or Z

    c. Rot X, Y, Z

    d. Rot in X or Y or Z

Certainly, you do not need the answers. It is so easy to watch the result instantaneously that it is much better for you to prove all your answers and change if the result does not satisfy you.

## Have a go hero - doing more

You know how easy it is to change the values of our cube. If the rotation is slower than you like, change it! And find the best result for you.

If the screenplay is empty and you need another object for reference, just add other cubes in the same scene. Select **Add | Mesh** and choose **Cube**, scale it by pressing *S* and move it around in your scene. Repeat this twice and try to move your cube characters without touching them. This is a good practice to see how you play games with the keyboard.

**Point of active view**

We did not discuss the view that we used in this chapter. In the games, we normally have various cameras. We will learn how to change this in *Chapter 5, Gameplay*. For the moment, the active camera is the active view in our **3D View**. For better understanding of how to move the cube, the **top view** is the active view of this game exercise.

# Summary

We have taken the first step in using the Blender Game Engine. It has not been so hard, has it? We have learned enough in this chapter, all of the secrets of logic bricks have been shown to you. You will find that you will use these same connections for setting up your first level of the game and again in your future projects of Blender Game Engine.

This chapter has covered a lot about the logic brick's world:

◆ We have learned the basics of the interface of Logic Editor. There are three parts of logic brick: sensors, controllers, and actuators. Each one has a sub-menu to choose the action that we want.

◆ We have seen how easy it is to connect them together. Draw a line between particular socket-like nodes, we can test all of the connections, a lot of trials, and perhaps some errors.

◆ Finally, we finished the whole movement of our player, a simple cube, making all of the necessary bricks move around, connecting and renaming them for best comprehensive multiple bricks.

We even play in the same point of view, but later we will change and it will improve our game.

Now, we are ready to forget the cube and create the character of our video game. If you are a good 3D modeler, you can choose to create your own character. Or to make it easier, get free characters from web libraries because you know that you can add this game logic to any model in Blender (no matter what shape or size it is), and it will move around just like the cube that we have learned to move!

# 2
# Your Characters

*You have seen that Blender's 3D game engine can be used to make and play computer games. In this chapter, I will explain how to go about designing your game and how to use Blender to get your model game characters, or 3D environments, to create casual video games.*

*If you're not good at making models, once you have tested how the character moves in the Blender engine, you can always download the model from the Internet and improve it later.*

In this chapter we shall:

- ◆ Learn how to create a library
- ◆ Involve enemies in the game
- ◆ Create a meeting point for the enemy and player

So let's get on with every single thing you want in the game; for example, storylines or levels of quests, characters, enemies, environments, interface designs, and so on.

So if you have your list of items and objects, it is time to decide how to get them.

## An example – save the whale!

We've got a basic idea of what characters are. Now, it's time sketch our character. If you're not good at drawing characters, try downloading them from the Internet.

For this book, I thought of a simple example for our game. Save the whale! We have drawn an easy character, a whale. We can create a fast-paced environment with a few icebergs, varied food of fish and seals, and we can create as many different enemies as we like, such as sharks, whale hunters, and pollution.

The game can augment its levels of difficulty as we develop our world using different environments. We can always increase the capability of your character with new keyboard functions.

Obviously, this is an example. Feel free to change the game, remake it, create another completely different character, and provide a gameplay of another gaming genre. There are thousands of possibilities, and it's fine if you deviate from our idea. It is important that you clear your design before you start your game library. That's all.

# How to create a library

If we start working with the **Blender Game Engine** (**BGE**), we must have a library of all of the objects we use in our game. For example, the basic character, or even the smallest details, such as the appearance of health levels of our enemies.

On the Internet, we can find plenty of 3D objects, which can be useful for our game. Let's make sure we use free models and read the instructions to run the model. Do not forget to mention the authorship of each object that you download.

Still, we know that we can open files in Blender and what needs to be imported. A few lines in the following section explain both these ways, step-by-step.

## Time for action – downloading models from the Internet

Let's go to one of the repositories for Blender, which can be found at `http://www.opengameart.org/`, and let's try to search for what is closest to our character.

1. Write `sea` in the **Search** box, and choose **3D Art** for **Art Type**, as shown in the following screenshot:

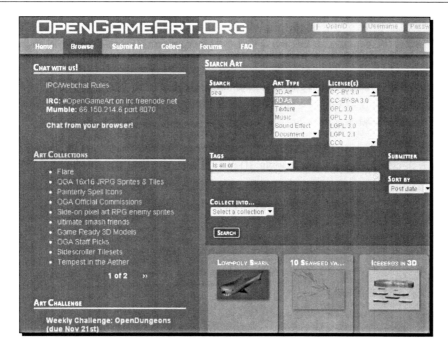

We have some interesting options. We see a shark, seaweed, and some icebergs to select from.

2. Choose and click on the thumbnail with the name **ICEBERGS IN 3D**:

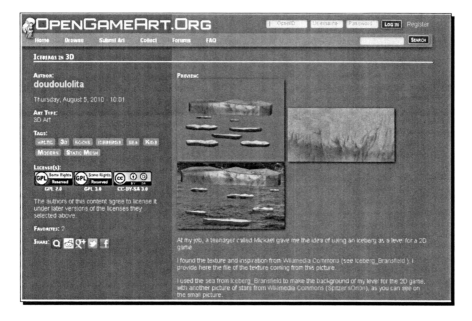

3. At the bottom of the page, you will find the `file.blend` downloadable. Click on it to start the download. We'll use this file later. Remember to click on RMB before the download begins.

4. Now, let's try web pages, which have libraries that offer 3D models in other formats. An example of a very extensive library is `http://sketchup.google.com/3dwarehouse/`.

5. Write `trawler` in the **Search** box, and choose the one that you like. In our case, we decided to go for the Google 3D model with the title **Trawler boat, 28'**:

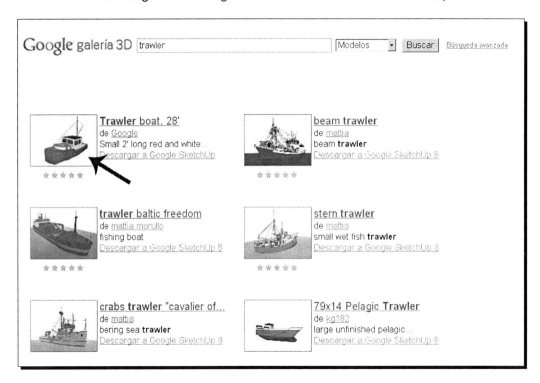

6.   Click on the **Download model** button:

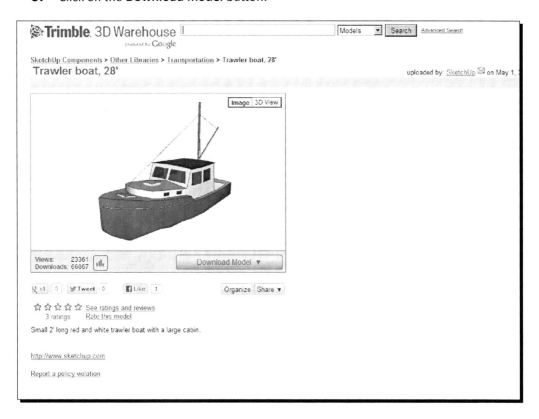

7.   Save the file on your hard disk, in a folder of your game.

## *What just happened?*

We have searched the Internet for 3D models, which will allow us to start a library for our game objects in Blender. Whether they are `.blend` files (original blender format) or of a 3D-model format, you can import them and work with them.

Don't download models that you will not use. The libraries on the Internet grow every day, and we don't need to save all of the models that we like. Remember that before downloading the model and using it, we need to check if it has a free license.

If you are releasing your project under some other free and/or open source license, then there could be licensing conflicts depending on what license the art is released under. It is your responsibility to verify the compatibility of the art license with the license you are using.

# Importing other files into Blender

Before the imported mesh can be used, some scene and mesh prepping in Blender is usually required. It basically cleans up the model imported in Blender.

**Google SketchUp** is another free, 3D software option. You can build models from scratch, and you can upload or download what you need, as you have seen. People all over the world share what they've made on the Google 3D Warehouse. It's our time to do the same.

Download the program from `http://sketchup.com` and install it. You can uninstall it later. Open the boat file in SketchUp, click on **Save as**, and export the 3D model using the **COLLADA** format.

The `*.dae Collada` format is a common, cross-platform file, which can be imported directly into Blender.

## Time for action – cleaning up the model in Blender

Open Blender and delete the cube using the *X* key and press the **OK** button in the pop-up menu. Go to **File | Import | Collada (.dae)** as seen in the following screenshot:

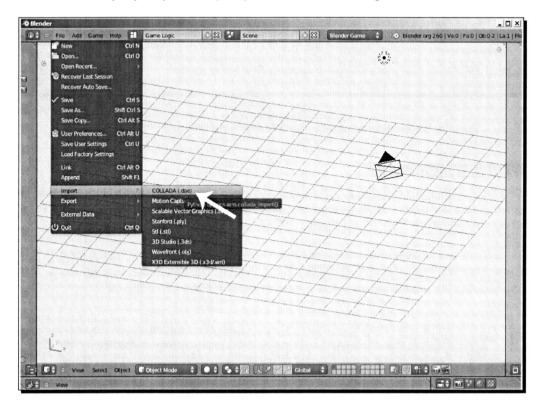

If you can't see the model in Blender, perform the following steps:

1.  Open up the **View Properties** panel from the 3D view, or press the *N* Key.

2.  Initially, the main parameter to be changed is in **View | Clip End**. The correct value is: `1000 (unit system)` or `25,4 (metric)` or `27,77 yd (imperial)`:

**3.** Scale the object using the *S* key, and center the axis on it:

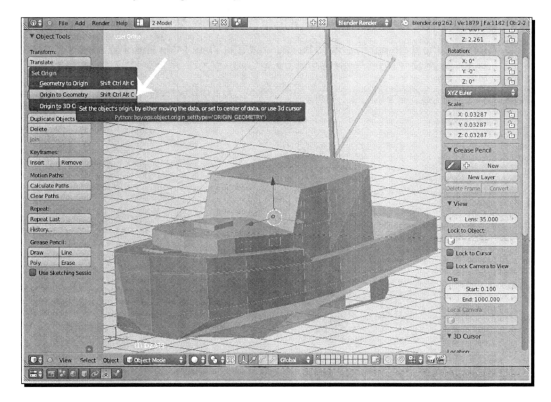

 On the **Object Tools** panel, click on **Origin | Origin to Geometry** before scaling the object.

**4.** Save the ship as a blend file, pressing **File | Save As**. Then, press the **Save As Blender file** button.

We will now attempt to design our main character: the whale.

**5.** Search for `killer whale` in a search box on the Web:

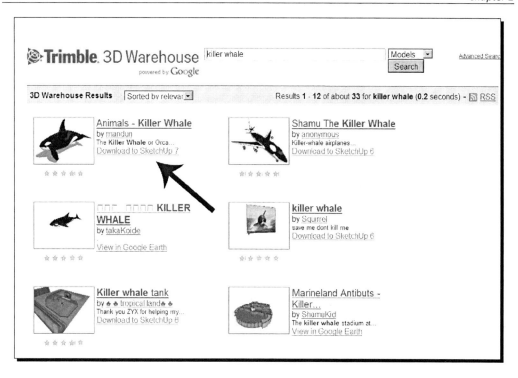

6. Click on the image titled **Animals - Killer Whale by mandun**, and the browser will open a new page. Click on the **Download** button, as shown in the following screenshot:

7.  Open Blender and press the *X* key to delete the cube. Choose **File | import | Collada (.dae)**, and select `killerwhale.dae` from your specific folder, if you previously exported it to the `collada` file. Repeat the steps we performed for the ship.

 If you prefer other formats, Blender can read 3Ds and `obj` files too. To see all formats, choose **File | User Preferences**, press on the **Addons** tab, and select the **Import/Export** button on the left menu.

## What just happened?

Getting 3D models with other types of extensions requires us to reset them and clean them so we can use them as Blend files. For this, we will import the model as explained previously. We have reduced the model, focused its axis, and taken everything that is not relevant for our model.

## Pop quiz – importing other files into Blender

1.  To add a 3D object library I need to:
    a.  Open the file
    b.  Import the file
    c.  Export the file

2.  To save a 3D object I need to:
    a.  Close the program
    b.  Close the original file
    c.  Save the file

3.  To clean the object, we must scale the model and set the axis in the:
    a.  Geometry to origin
    b.  Origin to geometry
    c.  Origin to the 3D cursor

## Have a go hero – growing the library

When you have a good library, try to import all models to the 3D view, and move and anchor each object on the scene. You will get a first impression of what your game looks like without any moving objects.

Remember that it is not necessary to find the exact model you need. Maybe some models closely resemble the model that you need. Perhaps, with simple modifications, your character can be ready. In the next paragraph, we will learn how to create a new model, but the tools we will use will be the same, as if you used a model from your own library.

# Involving enemies in the game

Let's start with our favorite game engine and put some objects on stage from our library. We can start by placing our whale, some icebergs here and there, and of course our main enemy: the fishing boat.

## Time for action – appending the enemy

It is recommended that you create a folder called `library`, and create subfolders under it, as your library grows. For example, under the `enemy` folder, you might want to create folders for animals, ships, food, and so on. If you have a good library with `.blend` files that has really neat objects used in it, then you can, from your current `.blend` file, link all of the objects into your current `.blend` file (level 01).

1. Choose **File | Append** and select the `ship` file. Press **Link Append File** by right-clicking on the **Library** button. The results will look like the following:

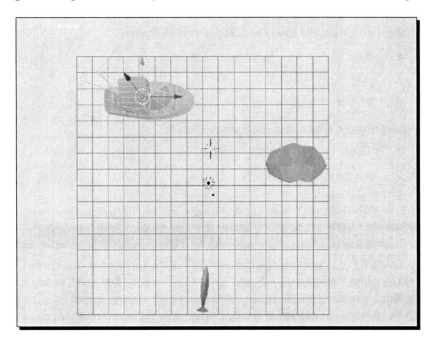

2. Work from the top, 3D view and select the enemy (ship). Scale it and move it as you like.

## What just happened?

We have placed the player, objects, and enemy in the top view, to give us a better understanding of the position of each element in the level we are preparing.

We use the **Append** option to import objects from the library. It allows us greater error correction if we want to modify any object at any moment.

If you use the **Linked** option, you cannot edit the object since all you have is a link to it. You cannot add to it or change it, because its source is in another file that is not open. However, you can modify the source, which will reflect in the linked blend files. This works very well for objects we want to share, which are not unique throughout the game.

## Pop quiz – Involving enemies in the game

1. For a complete library, we need to:
   a. Create a single folder
   b. Have several separate folders
   c. Sort objects in multiple folders

2. What extension should have the files for a clean library?
   a. `.dae`
   b. `.obj`
   c. `.blend`

3. To share objects, which files must we work with?
   a. `Insert`
   b. `Append`
   c. `Link`

## Have a go hero – reshaping the level

You already have a lot of information, which is required, to know what objects you need for each level of the game, and how you should apply them in your first level. In any case, we did not miss much emphasis on the measurements of each object, and as an example, our icebergs can be of many shapes and sizes. By changing its scale and rotation, you are bound to find plenty of possibilities with a single object. Remember that if you use the **Link** option, all of the original files in your `folders` libraries will be updated with iceberg-modifying sources. Learn your options and you will save a lot of time.

Try to move and reposition objects so that your player and the enemy can touch. However, you should reposition the objects again, if the battle overlaps the icebergs. With a few lines in the following section, we will see how the enemy moves, so be prepared!

# Creating a meeting point

We can try to move the ship around the whale, without ever having them collide with each other (for now). It is as if the enemy is waiting for the right time, and at the moment is only hovering near our player, waiting for one false move. So, let's create a loop of motion for our boat.

## Time for action – making the enemy follow a path

Use a plane to build a navigation mesh, where the boat does seem to surround the whale.

*1.* Choose **Add | Mesh | Plane**, and click on **Top 3Dview editor**. Press *S* to scale the plane:

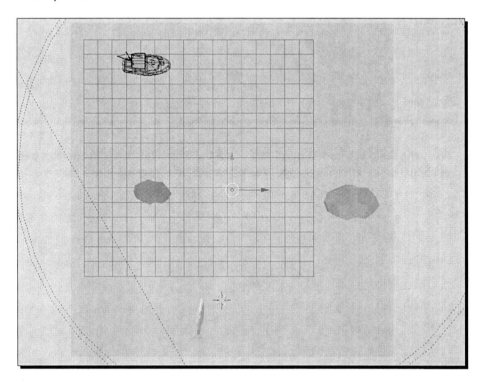

2. Press the *Tab key* to enter into the **Edit** mode, and subdivide the faces of the plane twice, as seen in the following screesnhot. Delete some faces around the icebergs, as our boat doesn't cross them:

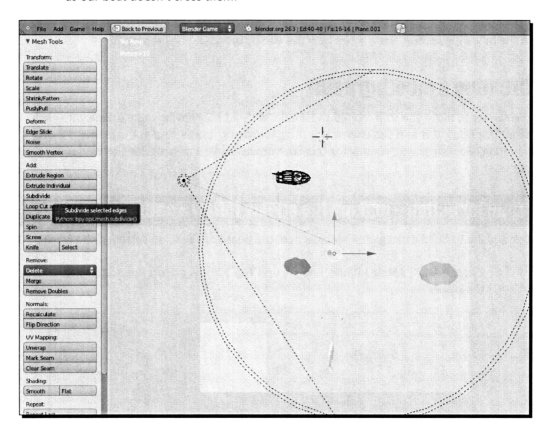

3. Press the **Build navigation mesh** button on the **Scene** tab in the **Properties** panel, as shown in the following image. The plane will be converted into a rainbow:

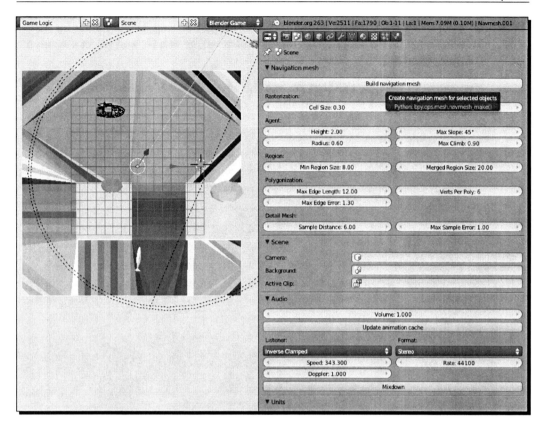

**4.** Go to **Logic Editor**, and choose **Always** as the value for **Sensors**. Add **And** for **Controllers**, and **Add** for **Actuators**, as shown in the following image:

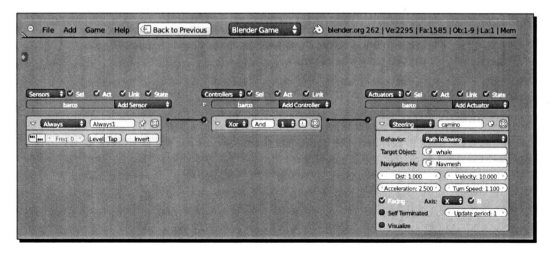

5. Connect them and choose another **Actuator** called **Steering**. The **Behavior** for **Steering** must be **Path following**. **Target Object** will be `whale`, and select `Navmesh` for **Navigation Me**.

6. If you want to see how the boat goes to the whale, select **Visualize** (a red line is seen when you press *P* to view in 3D):

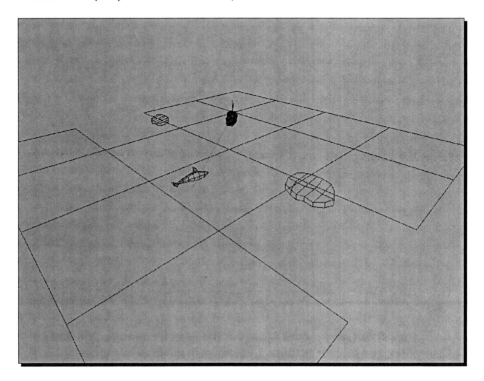

 Make sure our object ship is selected, before making these connections in the logic Bricks editor. If you have problems viewing the path, display the objects as a wire edge.

## *What just happened?*

Thanks to the logic bricks, we have an enemy encircling us in a part of the game. We must avoid this if we want to continue the game. Yet the behaviors are not complete, as we have not decided what to do if there is a collision.

As you have seen, it is very easy to give behaviors to the objects. One must know that sensors, controllers, and actuators must be used for this purpose.

We know how our enemy, the boat, moves without needing to press the keys on our keyboard. The boat stops when the navigation mesh ends.

## Pop quiz – creating a meeting point

1. To find the path of our enemy, which of the following options must we activate?

    a. Facing

    b. Self-terminated

    c. Visualize

2. The sensor must be activated when we select **Always** with which of the following?

    a. The whale

    b. The ship

    c. The plane

3. The navigation mesh option only works on:

    a. An object

    b. All objects

    c. A previous group of objects

## Have a go hero – more interactivity

If you have discovered how to fill the level of potential enemies, and know how they can move, try to make some changes to your player. For example, add one key for diving and passing under the boat or iceberg.

It depends on your imagination, and it will require a lot of attempts for this level of the game to be made more attractive.

# Summary

This chapter has provided us with resources for our game models. We learned that:

- The Internet is a great library of resources, but you do not always find what you're looking for. Several pages of models may give us some ideas to build our own object.

- If we have completed the library for our game objects, we are now ready to import it to the level that we are creating. We can begin to put more objects in our virtual world.

- With logic bricks, we can make the level of the game more interactive, encouraging only certain elements with the navigation mesh.

Well, it's time to create an entire first level for the game. We need to not only have our level map very clear, but also need to know where the player begins and ends the level. In the next chapter, we will look for ways to improve the quality level of the environment, to make it look fantastic in the game.

# 3
# The First Level

*If we continue with our example of an adventure in the Arctic, we could imagine a whale moving through a maze of icebergs. Your first level of play might be to find a way out for your whale. To do this, we put the whale at the beginning of our level, placing blocks of ice here and there. Finally, you need to know the way out of the first level that will take us to the next level.*

*To create a level for the player, we must know where to place the obstacles. Since this is a first level, with not much difficulty on battles and actions, we'll use it as tutorial-like level to get used to the game keys. Have you ever thought why almost all games begin the same way? It is almost a requirement, as in real life, that when you get to a new place you need to adapt yourself. You need to acclimatize, and I do not mean to just the cold made in the Arctic region.*

*Without realizing this, you have created a world, a quiet journey through the Arctic, but it still requires some light and other objects that recreate the atmosphere which characterizes this kind of level, with lots of little lights and textures.*

*For our whale, we will not put a sandy beach (for now). It will be a pack with some objects, such as the ice, a splendid sky, a solar light that illuminates everything, and water.*

In this chapter we will learn how to:

- Block out a level environment
- Create a player view
- Define the boundaries
- Construct the end-level zone

So, let's get on with each theme.

# Block out a level environment

We can start with something simple, such as standard platform games with a side view, so we can get an idea of the journey we must undertake to reach our goal.

If you like platform games, start by putting the player to the left, so we know where to begin. Let's put some icebergs in the middle and give an end to the level, such as a door or an arc of ice the whale must cross. That's the end of the level.

## Time for action – creating the scene

Let's put our whale on the right side of the screen, and let's make sure that we are working on the right lateral view.

1.  Press 3 on the numpad, or select **Right** from the **View** menu, as shown in the following screenshot:

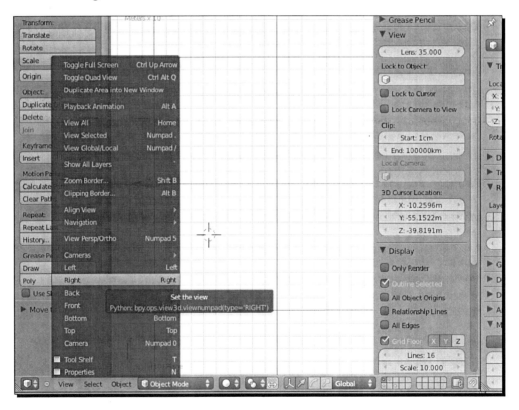

When pressing the numpad key, the mouse cursor must be on the **Target 3D** view to see a concrete view.

2. Choose **File | Append**, to select the whale `blend` file from your library, as shown in the following screenshot. Put the whale in the left-middle corner:

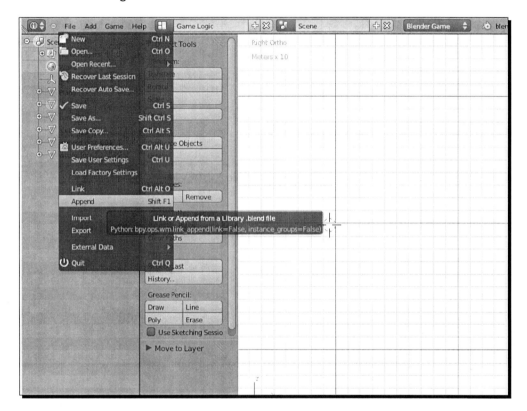

Select the whale object from the object folders available in the `blend` file library.

**3.** The Y-axis is displayed in green. Align the center of whale on the Y-axis, as shown in the next screenshot. The green line can be used for a reference between the depth of the sea and the sky:

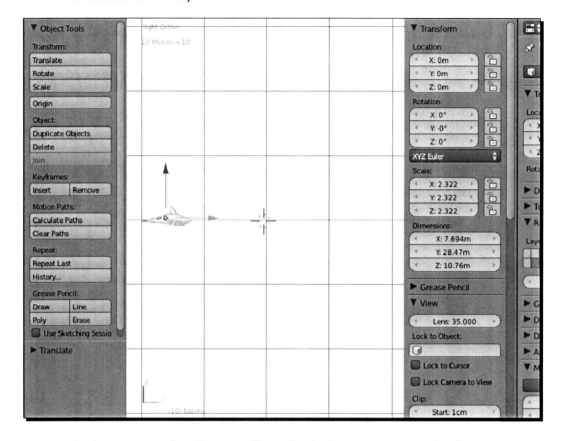

For better comprehension, we will use the Y-axis to represent sea level.

4. Repeat the same operation for different blocks of ice. Choose **File | Append**, to select the iceberg blend file from your library. Feel free to put them where you think they will be most convenient. If you want to duplicate an iceberg, choose **Duplicate Objects** from the **Object Tools** panel on the left of your screen, or use the shortcut *Shift + D* combination and drag it to the right place, using the *G* key:

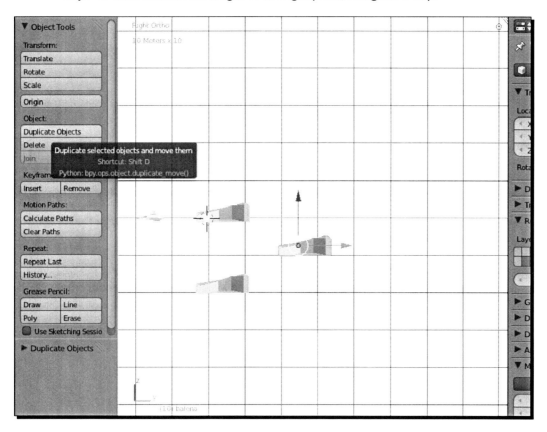

**5.** We need the icebergs with a relative size scale in front of our whale. Scale the iceberg, making a cool muzzle, which would look similar to the next image. Select the object and press the *S* key to determine how big or small you want it to be. After the *S* key is pressed, you can press another key (for the Y- or Z-axis) to determine which axis you want to increase or decrease the dimensions of your object.

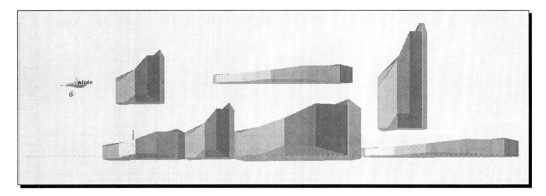

Don't just try the *S* key to scale the iceberg, also try the *R* key to rotate the iceberg. This displays another, different angle of the iceberg!

**6.** Once relocated, the icebergs should be positioned as shown to you in the following screenshot. Let's go to **Logic Editor** to edit the logic bricks and move our whale, like how we moved the cube in *Chapter 1, Things You Need to Know*.

Select the whale with the **Right Mouse Button** (**RMB**), to operate with logic bricks. Press the right arrow key in the blank cell with no label if , for example, you want to move the whale to the right. Click on **Add And** as the value for **Controller**, click on **Add** as the value for **Actuators**, and choose **Motion**. Change the value of **x-box** to 0.20 in **Loc** (location). We will now connect these blocks systems together. Click-and-drag from the socket (small circle) at the end of **Sensors**, to the socket at the start of **Controllers**, and again to the **Actuators** brick. Repeat this operation for the rest of the arrow keys.

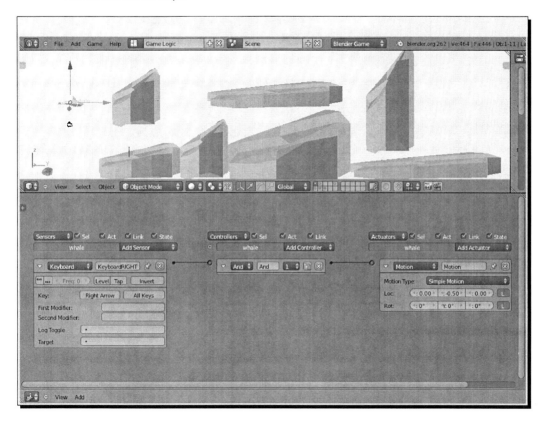

**7.** Test your game. Try to move the whale from the beginning to the end of the game. At the moment, there aren't any collisions. We will learn how to create them later. The important thing now is that our player can move freely through the icebergs.

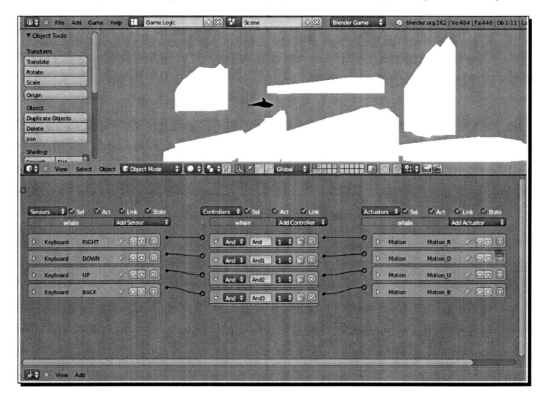

The values of this project to move the whale are as follows:

◆ The right arrow key, to move the player forward, is `Y= -0.50`. This value depends on how fast the whale moves in the forward direction.

◆ The left arrow key, to move the player back, is `Y= 0.10`. This value is smaller, as the whale is slower when it moves backwards, as compared to forward movement

◆ The down arrow key, to move the player down, is `Z= -0.30`. This value depends on how fast the whale moves down when we move it.

◆ The up arrow key, to move the player up, is `Z= 0.40`. The value is increased, when compared to the downward movement, because the whale swims upwards faster.

## *What just happened?*

From this exercise we learned to design and redesign our level of play, so the player has a specific route. Our ideas evolved as we tried the game, and we saw that we may need to move certain objects so the player can move easily. This task of repositioning our player environment gave us our first glimpse of how each thing will inevitably be remodeled as we put it into our game. Thanks to BGE, this verification process is immediate.

We have created the start of the game, and we have placed our obstacles so our player moves as if he were inside a maze. Measuring the exact position of each object is what takes longer. Once you relocate and test everything again, you could have an accurate idea of how the level is going.

## Pop quiz – blocking out a level environment

1. It is very easy to assume that everyone thinks like you, but the game needs to have other options according to different people's requirements. If you want to create a double-jump motion, which local axis must you change?

    a. X

    b. Y

    c. Z

2. Which brick will you choose if you want to limit the water's surface as if it were up to where you can get your character?

    a. Sensor

    b. Controller

    c. Actuator

3. Which key do you need to make a whale jump?

    a. The *J* key

    b. The *Space bar*

    c. It doesn't matter

## Have a go hero – doing it better

Would it not be better if the whale dives minimally rotated, as if it has bowed its head and thus improve the movement of the player?

How about trying to modify the necessary connections in the logic bricks for the whale and its tail, so it can resurface almost vertically?

So, you've seen how easy it is to build a labyrinth. In this example, we have proposed one way of doing it. Why not create two possible routes in your game to be at the same place? This will make it much more interesting! As not all players choose the same way to make the character move, if you create multiple possible solutions, the game wins in visual richness and alternatives.

Find a suitable site in your game and create two or three possibilities to trap the character and make it retrace its steps. In a maze, everyone knows what might happen if you take a chance. At this level of your game, make a maze full of possibilities.

# Creating a player view

You may not realize it, but you created a map level recently when you finished the previous exercise. The only way to create a new map is to modify what we have done before. But first, we suggest you get a name to our scene. How do we do that? Let's see this and more. From here on, we will start creating new cameras, new scenes, and of course, new layers that overlay it.

## Time for action – renaming the scene

The first thing to make clear is that the **3D Viewport Right** view leaves us with a complete vision of our labyrinth, right? This view must be the map view, and we need to add a closer look to follow our player.

We will create a new camera, which will only show a part of our labyrinth, and move the whale. The camera too should move at the same time.

1.  Split in two views, the 3D view would look similar to the following screenshot. Drag it from the upper-right corner of the window to the left, and you will have two areas. The left area is for **3D Viewport**, called the **Right** view, and we modify the right area for a view of the camera (key *0*):

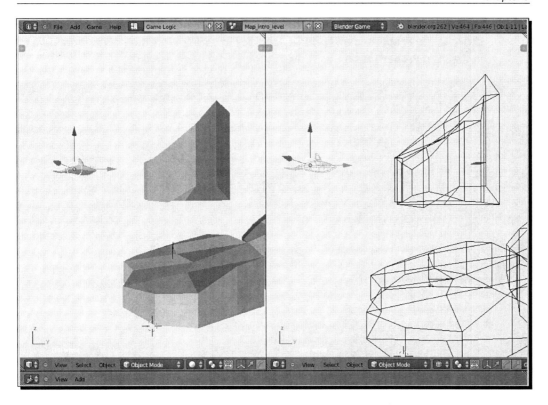

2.  Our scene even has a default camera. Now, let's add a new camera to the scene. To do that, go to the **Main** menu and select **Add | Camera**.

**3.** Let's rename the newly created camera while we are at it. To do so, hit the *N* key to show up the **Property** panel on the right. Key in `Camera1` as the new camera name, in the **Item Properties** box, as shown in the following screenshot:

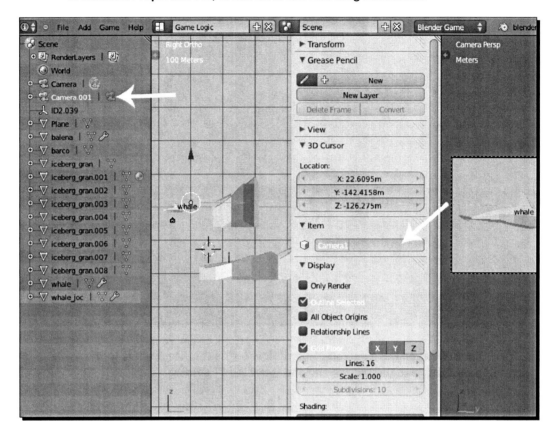

The default camera is called `camera` and the second one is called `camera.001`. Don't confuse them or change the names. Be sure that `Camera.001` is now `Camera1` and is selected! You can see the different names of the objects in the outliner.

4.  Set `Camera1` while you are in the **Right** view of **3D Viewport**. Bring it closer to our whale. Let's put on the **Logic Bricks** editor and make the connections:

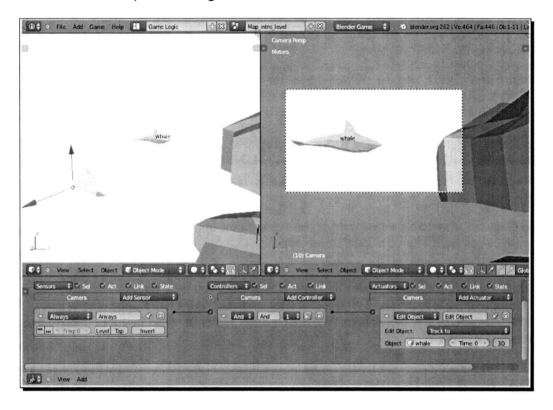

5.  Add **Always** as the value for **Sensor**, and add **And** as the value for **Controllers**. Then, add **Edit Object type** as the value for **Actuators**, which you can select it from the pop-up menu.

6.  To see the difference between the two cameras, change the value of **Edit object** to **Track to**, and select `whale` in the cell object that is empty. Press the **3D** button to enable the camera if you see that **Track** is set to `whale`. Before finishing the blocks, connect them and press *P* to see the results.

## *What just happened?*

We have made a substantial improvement, which is quite important at our level of play. By just putting a camera much closer to the player we have defined the field of view for our player, and we have created some intrigue in the maze. Where do you move if you cannot see the maze completely?

With a new camera, we have created the sensor called `Always` in the logic brick editor, which is constantly connected to our object that follows the whale by the actuators called `Track to`.

### Have a go hero – creating the real map view

Hey, wait! We have the ability to have a minimap overlay on top of the game view by reusing the actual full map view. I wish to see a map, but I don't see it. I just see a simple view.

In *Chapter 5*, *Gameplay*, we will explain the overlays. The important thing is to have the map view. Do you want a hero? Make a closer map view to zoom in, and the user will have two maps to choose from.

But if you really want to improve this proposal, why don't you try a first-person camera, a camera that is above the head of your character, and maybe give him a point of view more effective than the one shown here. Why not try other camera anchors that are bound to find one that is better.

# Defining the boundaries

We think we have covered a lot. We said we had the full level, but it is not quite true. We still have two dilemmas ahead: starting and finishing the game. Take a moment to see how the beginning of the game is to be created.

We have assumed that the player will begin to go forward, but we have also said it was important to cover all possibilities. What if the player decides to go back just to start? We will also cover that possibility. Are you one of those players who prefer to explore the environment before they start playing the game? Ahem! No comments about it except that we have a problem now—not you, dear reader, but the potential options. We should cover any possible way out. We must force the whale to go forward, and it should have no other choice but to go in a particular direction.

# Time for action – closing the entry point

As mentioned earlier, if we decide to imitate a platform game, you should close the left side of the screen by adding a wall of ice behind the entry point. Let's do it.

**1.** Select an iceberg, choose **Menu Object | Duplicate Linked** to create another object, and scale it to your preferred size:

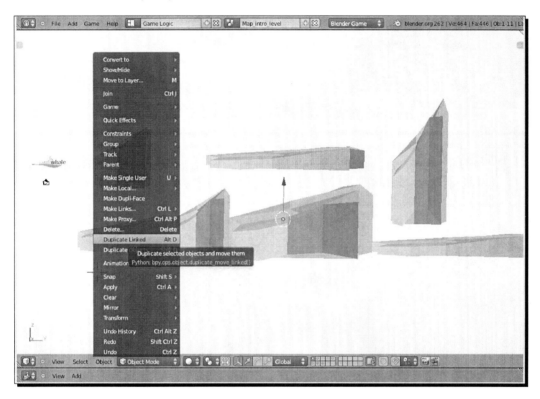

We choose **Duplicate Linked** to create a new object with all of its data linked to the original object. If you modify one of the linked objects in **Edit Mode**, all linked copies are modified. Don't use the **Duplicate** option, please. If you rotate the original, the copy remains unchanged. This means the transform properties are copies and not links.

2. Move the new duplicate object as shown in the following image, and close the entry. If necessary, duplicate other icebergs to make a perfect corner with no exit:

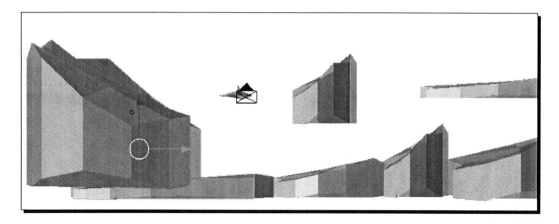

3. Add a cube for the virtual sea and scale it to be as big as you want, as shown in the following screenshot:

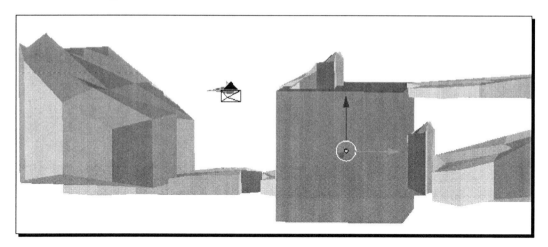

The most important thing is the line at the top of the sea. In our case, we put the cube in the middle and resize it so the tops of icebergs are seen, as shown in the following screenshot:

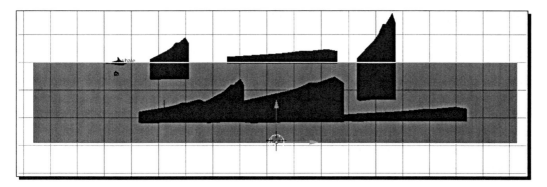

4.   Make a wire type in the `display` property to see the whale, or press the *Z* key. In fact, this is not important now, but you can see the limits of our whale. Delete the cube if you cannot see the whale.

Another screenshot of our virtual sea is as follows:

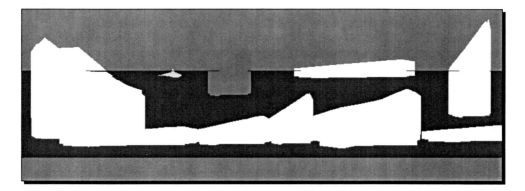

## What just happened?

We have doubled some icebergs close to the start of the game, providing the whale with a single point of exit ahead of it. We have scaled and rotated the objects to get a better contrast with the rest, and finally we have simulated the sea surface line to see how the objects are placed in the game.

The sea will be dynamic, so we need not worry about it for the time being. As we said before, it is just used to simulate the placement of the objects and the surface line. We can delete it once we have seen our ceiling boundary.

## Have a go hero – experimenting with the start of the game

You've seen how to improve the main entrance with the same objects you have on stage.

Why not place a ship wreck, or something that is not a part of the game, which can provide a stunning visual impact for the player? Remember that the details are as important as the actions we perform. If we have a very observant player, he would appreciate that since being in your game, he can sometimes see things that enhance the view. This also tells a story through background details, without needing words. Why not use this hint as a good starting point to explore your visual creativity?

# Marking the end of level

It is clear that the end should always be encouraging. Try to create something that makes the player thinks he has discovered something really wonderful. The final chapter should be memorable. It is time to create the end of our game, and since we created a great start, why should we not create a glorious end? We will refer to our objects, and perhaps our library. If we find something interesting, we will use it to create the end of this level.

## Time for action – opening the end point

Imagine the end of your circuit. At the end of a tedious maze, find a way out, perhaps a hole to escape through. There are many ways out, and there are some spectacular options too. Why not pick one of them? In this case, we will create an arc of ice.

Crossing under an arc is like crossing through a door, a starting point, something we could use to go to the start point again and continue the conquest. Here, just as our player crosses the goal, we use the logic brick and almost magically arrange it, so you can load the next level.

1. Make an arc of ice with icebergs, as shown in the following screenshot:

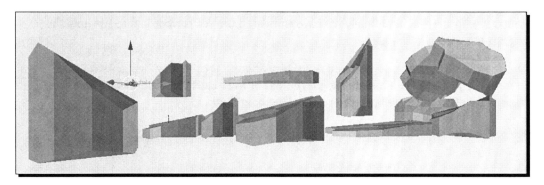

A close-up view shows how the icebergs are located.

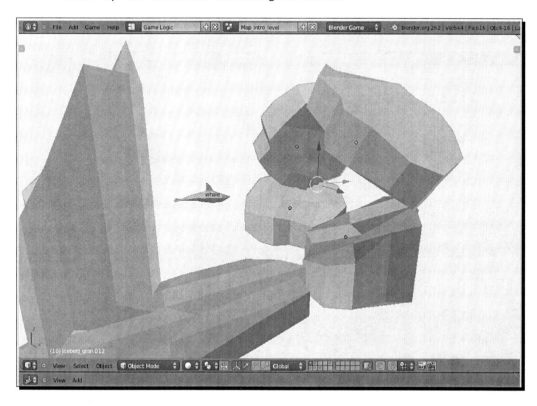

2. Add a plane in the middle of the arc, as shown in the following screenshot. Press the *N* key and rename it to Endlevel1 in the **Item Properties** box.

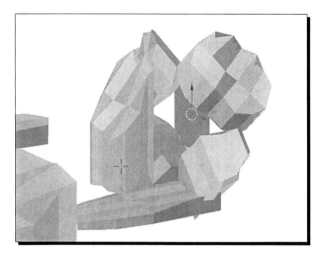

3.  Go to the **Logic Bricks** editor, select **Collision** as **Sensors**, add **And** as **Controllers**, and finally choose **Scene** from **Menu** in **Add actuators** as **Actuators**, as shown in the following screenshot:

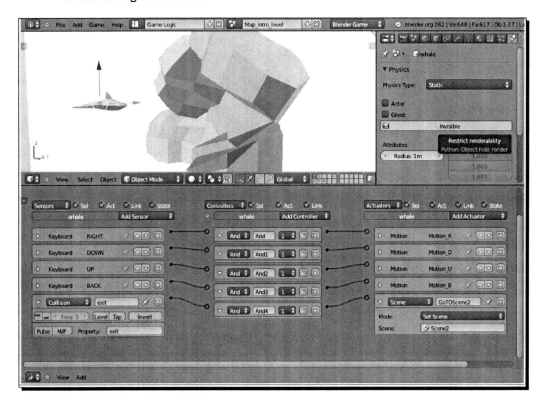

4.  Add a new scene and rename it as `Mapintrolevel` or `Scene2`. Go back to the previous scene and write `exit` as the value of the property for the sensor, as shown in the following screenshot. Make the connections.

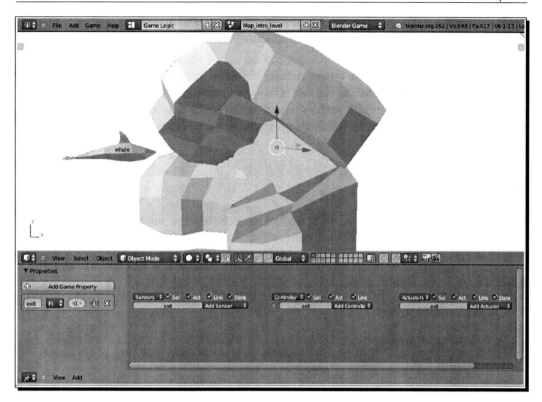

5. To add custom properties for additional objects, go to the **Properties** panel of the selected object, and press the **Add Game Properties** button. Press the + button and change the name. The properties are ready to use. Press the *X* button if you want to delete it.

## What just happened?

The end is much more technically developed than the beginning. As you saw, we need to create a scene to justify specific loading of the second level, as long as the player reaches the goal.

When the whale touches the plane (make it invisible by checking the **Invisible** button box option in the **Properties** panel) with the property level set to exit, stage two will be displayed.

## Have a go hero – changing the end point

If you want to explore the result of different collisions, test the example game that we have created by changing the collision sensor to **Near** or **Radar**. You need a sensor to determine how close the object is to reaching the end. Change of scene is easy if you create a new scene first. Try the other options, such as restarting the scene or level, because we currently do not have a second level. This option brings us closer to the process of changing levels so the screen does not stay blank.

# Summary

We have learned much in this chapter, as we had an entire level to practice. Now, we will only refine what we created, and we are not even halfway through the book, remember that!

Improving the game is what will take you more time. Be patient, and rebuild what we've learned here, if you wish to do so.

Specifically, we have covered:

- **Creating an environment**: Creating an entire level lets us know how and where to put of all our objects, how to interact with our players, and especially how to resize the environment.

- **Making a view**: Glops! We made the level map before we made a first-person view! So, we have prepared the point of view for seeing the map in *Chapter 5*!

- **Start point**: Making a good start is worth the effort, right? Sometimes the simplest things are better than the details. If we do not neglect good presentation, you can bet it will be maintained throughout the game.

- **End point**: Make a final softer than initially thought. Every level needs to be impressive, but sometimes, not all of them need to explode in the air. A spectacular environment setting also gives good results, although here the logistics plays an important role, as you know.

Since we have learned how to use the change of level or end of a game level, we are prepared to modify the player in any of these possibilities. We know how to restart the game, how to reset the player, and how to transfer keys. Do you want to animate the sea in which the whale swims? All of this and more is explained in the next chapter. So, have a cup of tea or a coffee, and continue with the exciting next chapter!

# 4
# Collisions

*The most exciting part when creating a game is when your brother, or perhaps a friend, is able to move the character in your game through the entire stage. However, this interactivity is not complete if the character does not respond to certain automatic responses, called collisions.*

**Collisions** *are the most important part of our character's interaction with the universe in which it moves. This collision between the character and everything around it is important in the* **Blender Game Engine** *(***BGE***). There are* **Static collisions** *that set up by default, but if you need a response from the object and not from the character, you must use a type of collision called* **Dynamic physics***, in BGE. We have a virtual world where we cannot move through walls, mountains, and objects (such as blocks, doors, and in our case, the icebergs). It is logical that any wall will stop the adventure of our character, which will need to change the direction if it needs to move on. But there comes a time in the game when we need to move those blocks, slide them, or if relevant, make them vanish. Anyone who has played video games knows what I mean.*

We are going to explain some of the most common responses of these types of collisions, which are listed as follows:

- ◆ Respawning the character
- ◆ Creating trap doors
- ◆ Natural motion: rolling rocks
- ◆ Creating looped actions

So, let's get on with each theme.

# Respawning the character

Racing games are the best example to understand why we need to create this ability. When the car leaves the track, it automatically restores its position within the circuit. In simple terms, this is possible because the length and height of the track are invisible walls. If the car collides with the invisible walls around the road, it returns to the track. This is logical, isn't it? Then, let the logic brick create this response to the collision.

## Time for action – returning to the original position

Reopen the last exercise where we made the whale cross an arc of icebergs to reach the end of the first level of the play. Remove all of the icebergs to make it easier to understand and work on this exercise. We will only allow the whale and the plane to be displayed. When the player touches the plane, the whale returns to its initial position.

*1.* Go to **File**, and click on **Append**. Add a new iceberg:

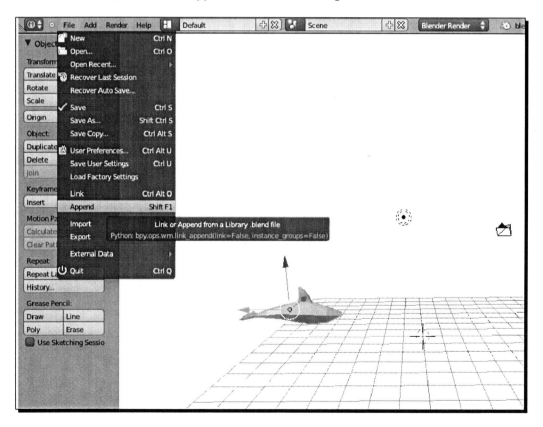

**2.** Choose **Game Logic** as the screen layout, and click on the whale to select it. You must see the whale marked in the **Logic Editor** panel:

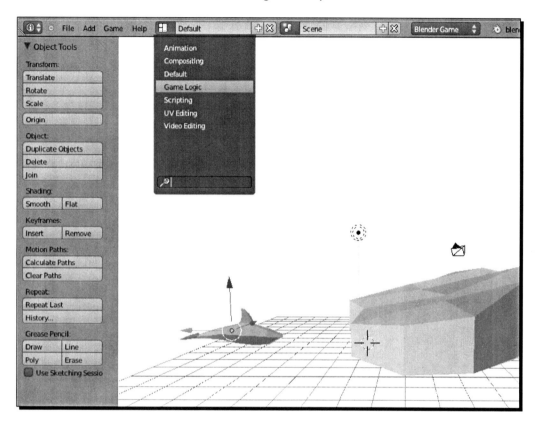

 Remember to choose **Blender Game** as the engine to use the rendered scene.

**3.** Select the whale and click **Add Sensor** to choose a sensor called **Touch**. You will also see the **Keyboard** sensors that were made for moving the whale (refer to *Chapter 1, Things You Need to Know*, to see how they were created):

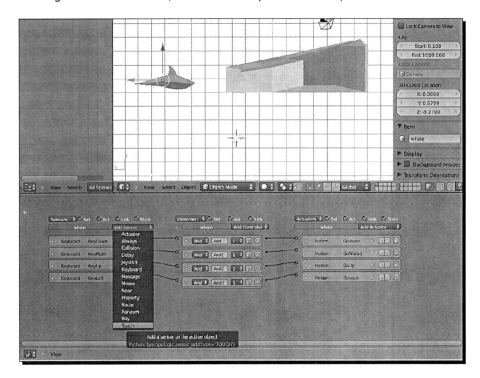

 We use the **Touch** sensor when the object is in contact with another object without the needed properties. A **Collision** sensor works like a **Touch** sensor, but we can also filter by property as we saw in the previous chapter.

**4.** Select an actuator, choose **Motion**, and change the value of **Y** to -0.50 in **Loc** (check if the Y-axis is the correct direction in which the whale should move, and if not, change the value as required). Connect the bricks directly:

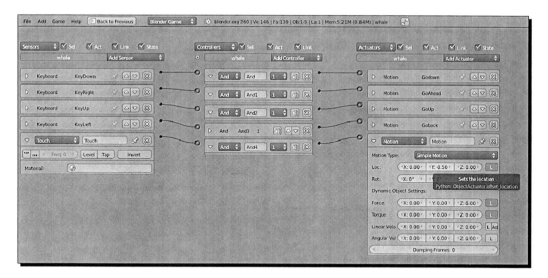

 If you don't add a controller, but connect a sensor to an actuator (left brick to right brick), it will automatically add the **And** controller (middle brick). You'll be skipping a step.

**5.** Press *P*, after you click on the 3D view and test the collision. If the whale doesn't return to the position, make sure **Physics Type** is set to **Dynamic** (see the **Physics** properties tab, select the whale, and choose **Dynamic**), as shown in the following screenshot:

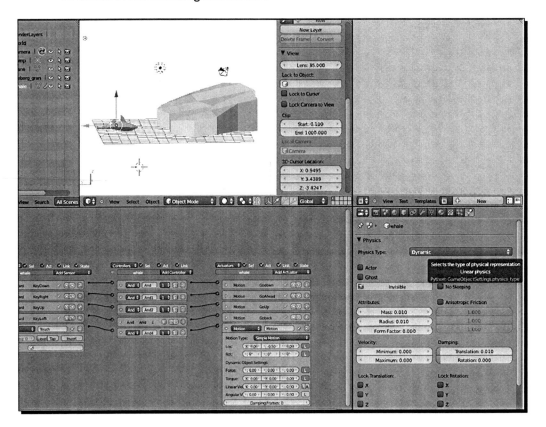

 Change the rotation value for a better comprehension and visibility of the **Touch** sensor. If it's ok, delete the rotation value after the test.

An observation: the applications of forces and speeds that are not dynamic objects will have no effect. They are not evaluated by the game engine and are considered fixed on the scene perfectly, as they only move the objects in new positions or specific angles. To generate a collision response, we must not only take into account the mass and friction of the object, but also that the object is marked as a dynamic type.

# What just happened?

Starting from the end, we wanted the whale to interact with the world around it. For testing, we placed our character and an object to help us interpret a barrier (a big iceberg or whatever) which makes the character go back to the position where it was. To do this, we had to change the type of physical play and adjust to dynamic. Thus, we can get contacts, and our character collisions with other objects can be calculated to give the answer that we assign. In the previous exercise, the whale returned to the old position it was in before the collision.

## Pop quiz – respawning the character

1. If you want to create a collision, which object has the connection in the logic brick?
   a. The whale
   b. The iceberg
   c. Both

2. Which sensor would you choose if you wanted to make a crash?
   a. Collision
   b. Touch
   c. That is immaterial

3. Which type of collision needs an object response?
   a. Static
   b. Dynamic
   c. Doesn't matter, it only affects the player

## Have a go hero – doing it better

There are many possibilities for creating collisions. We can use distance, as we did in the example, but can we also create a change in direction (for example, when using a ball or returning the character to a specific point of the stage, perhaps a check point).

If we are in a forest, some trees may be in the path of our character and others may not. It is much easier to apply a material to certain objects that we want our character to react to, and therefore not create actions for the logic bricks of other objects. Although this material may not be seen, it is perfectly useful for collisions of the objects with the material, regardless of the type of the object that you see (including if we want this object to be invisible to our player). Try choosing a specific material in a box of a sensor brick. You can see that the character reacts to only the object that has collided with the material you specified.

The easiest feature for a response to a collision outside the game is to reload the game. Try the **Game Actuator** logic brick. This is really intuitive handling.

For good practice with these types of collisions, we suggest you try to "knock out" the character for a moment to return to the game in a few seconds. Maybe a couple of spins on the same axis could be a clue.

# Creating trap doors

I believe there is no platform game where we will not, sooner or later, open an access door or other place, by opening what initially could not be accessed. The simple idea of this new exercise is to show how areas seemingly cannot be accessed by the character (initially), and how we can create a new access path through openings or doors that were previously closed.

## Time for action – moving the blocks of ice

I do not think there are many doors in the Arctic, and fewer under water. Let's substitute the doors for blocks of ice. These will move in some way to prevent the whale access elsewhere. To do this, we must finish the previous example.

Before you begin, we need to move the trap iceberg when the whale approaches or leaves it. The icebergs that blocked the way will remain fixed in their positions.

1.  To create a new file, delete the box, and then click on **File | Append** to select your library (the whale and three icebergs) for our exercise, as shown in the following image. Rename the middle iceberg to `iceberg_son`, which will serve as the trapdoor.

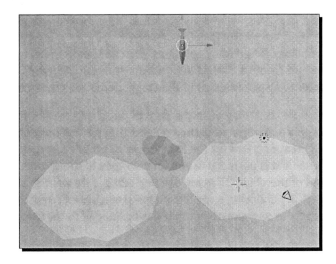

[  Scale the middle iceberg down so that it is smaller than the rest. This will be used as the trap door. ]

**2.** Change the window from **Logic Editor** to **Graph Editor**, and move the door iceberg a little bit to the left, as shown in the following screenshot:

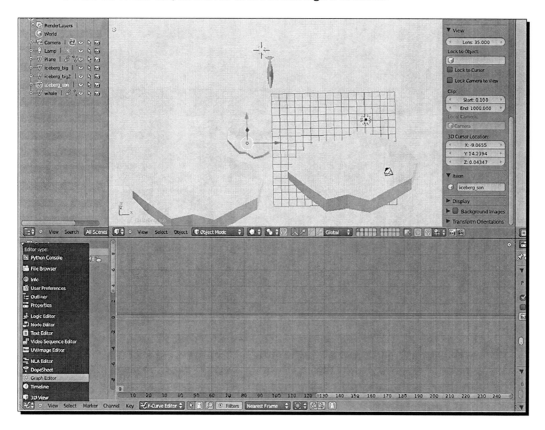

**3.** Go to **Menu**, choose **Key**, and select **Insert Keyframe** or press the *I* key. Move the slider of **Timeline** to frame 30, and press *I* again, to insert another keyframe:

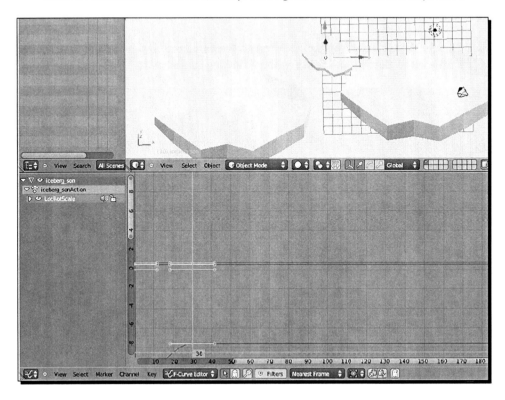

You can see a list of new channels which were automatically created with the name of the selected object and the suffix Action. This is a register of the curve of the animation. When we press the *I* key, the Keyframe is marked by one dot in the curve graphic. Come back to the **Logic Editor** window, and add a new sensor called **Near** for the door iceberg:

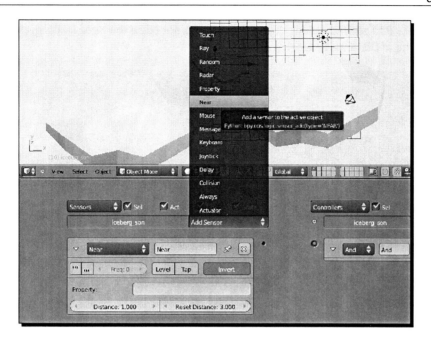

4. Add **And** as the value for **Controller**, and then similarly add **Action** as the value for **Actuator**. Connect them after selecting the action of the drop-box menu, in this case, iceberg_sonAction. You can also select the start and end of frames of your animation on the respective boxes:

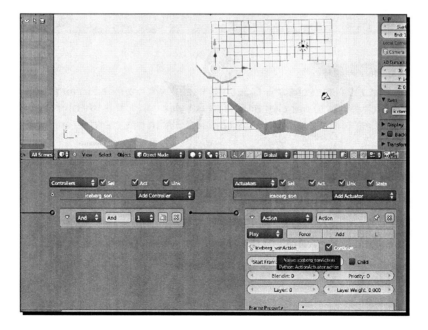

**5.**  Press *P* to see the results. If the sensor does not close the door iceberg, change the value of **Distance** to **Near**:

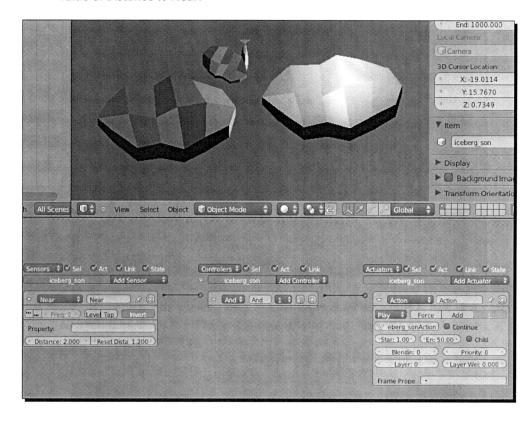

## What just happened?

We have seen that the **Near** sensor is especially useful when applied to an action of our environment which reacts to our character, and not vice versa. It is the object of the scene that reacts according to the position of the character. With this exercise, we have learned to:

- Create a new sensor called **Near**
- Create a simple animation with the F-curve
- Apply this animation to the Blender game
- Create a versatile actuator called **Action**
- Define some of the frames of the animation we see when two objects interact
- Check the area of influence of the new sensor

## Have a go hero – the more, the better

Come on, don't tell me you have not seen the number of options available to the **Action** actuator. They are incredible. Ping-pong and loops may seem like a wonder to you. Try it with this exercise, it may suit you best for what you need.

Finally, we stopped to comment that fortunately the sensor is near the **Invert** function. Why not go further and try placing another iceberg to activate the access door? Perhaps, with a limiter clock run to make it more interesting with a time limit. Good luck!

# Real-time motion

An object in a ramp could be affected by physics, and it must have gravitational acceleration. Each object that is an actor has mass and size variability. In conjunction with the frame rate, Blender uses this info to calculate how fast the object should accelerate downward in the game.

## Time for action – rolling objects

Let's test what would happen if we met with a detachment of ice. The pieces would roll into the water and dive deep into the ocean. Reflected in this sentence, there are too many laws of physics. We will split the iceberg and will be left with only the pieces of iceberg rolling down a slope. Let's see how the game engine calculates this movement.

*1.* Select an iceberg, choose **Object**, and duplicate the link six times to create other objects. Scale and rotate them, as shown in the following screenshot:

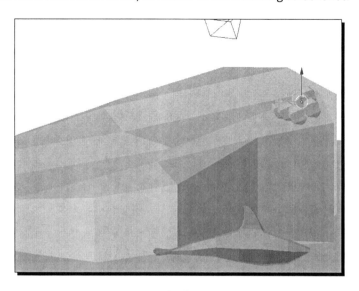

2. Select each one of little icebergs and repeat this operation: select **Dynamic** in the **Physics Properties** tab, as follows:

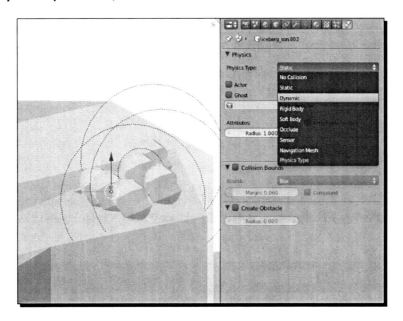

3. Activate the **Collision Bounds** option and set it to **Sphere**, in each iceberg:

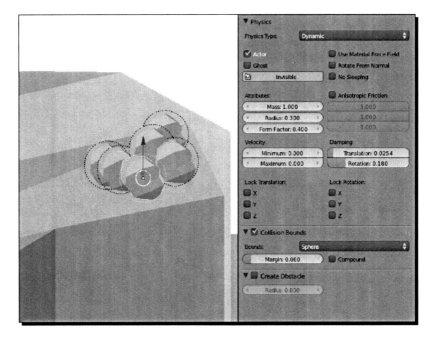

The radius (marked with a circle of dots) of influence in **Attributes** is 0.3 in this case. You must change it to fit your version of the scaled iceberg!

**4.** Press P to see the result. If you don't like it, change Velocity to Maximum, and try it again. Changing values a little bit changes the results of a simulation, a lot. In the following image, the rocks are moving down:

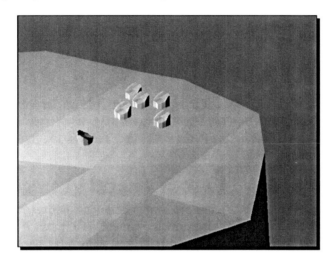

# What just happened?

We have seen that the simulation of gravity has its effect on the game. First, and most important, is to find the physical values determined for each object.

Remember the steps we have followed:

1. We have applied the type of object (several small icebergs) in Dynamic.
2. We have activated the option **Actor** as the player of the action.
3. We have remarked that a sphere must be set as the collision type in the collision bounds.
4. We have modified the values of the radius of action.
5. We have changed the speed of each object.

Most importantly, although we have not mentioned it before, there will be physical consequences of small icebergs sliding down a slope. Always keep in mind the surface and its inclination. Any modification has great effects on the physical state of objects.

Now that you know that each object can have its properties and can change the value, you can test the physics involved by not to applying the same values for all of the rocks. For example, a bigger rock reacts differently from the one that is not so big.

If you dare, you could include an obstruction, which does not affect all of the objects in the middle of the fall, and reacts differently for each object. Finally, just to see the results for yourself, try rolling many icebergs to the end of the cliff and into the water. The diving simulation achieved is spectacular!

# Creating looped actions

In the previous example, we talked about the fall of objects, but we did not mention anything about where they fall. So, let us turn our attention to creating water, since all of these icebergs through which our whale is floating, are in the water. Let's see how to simulate this effect.

There are many ways to create water. The movement of fluids is not recommended to generate waves. Therefore, let's turn to texture movement, as it makes it appear as if the water moves. With the BGE, we can use several different techniques, depending on the final texture mode. In this case, it only works with GLSL.

1. Make a plane by going to **Menu | Add | Mesh | Plane**. Scale it as you like, and apply a cloud texture twice, as `water1` and `water2`, as follows:

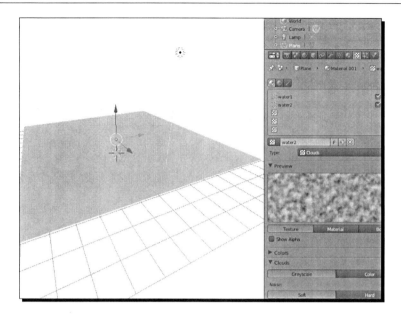

 The **Cloud** texture is one of a list of the available procedural textures that give an overall irregularity to the material, to look like the sea.

**2.** Increase the size value of **water2** a little bit, to 0.35, to see the difference between the two water objects with the same texture:

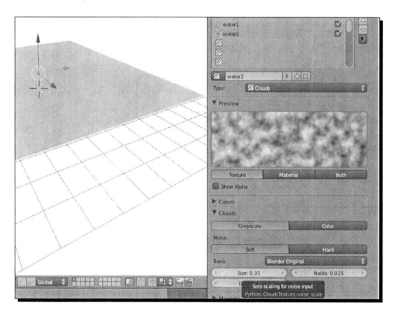

**3.** Add a last layer with an image file of a JPG water texture (we use the one downloaded from the Internet by typing `water texture free` in the **Search** navigation).

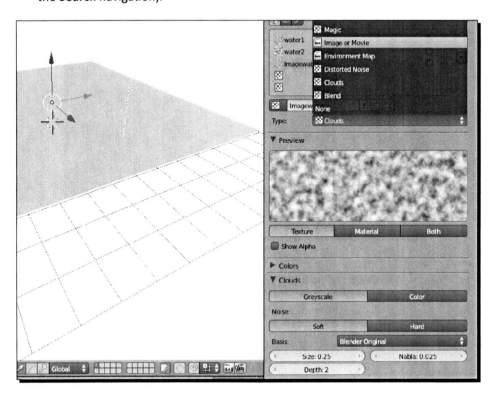

**4.** Go to the **Modifiers** tab and select **Displace**:

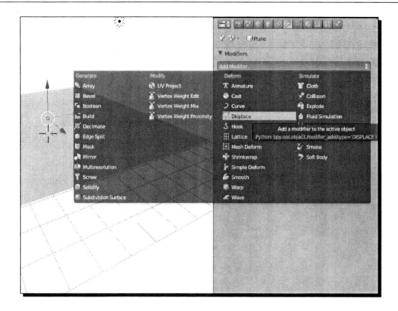

> The **Displace** modifier displaces the vertices in a mesh, based on the intensity of a texture.

5. Change to **Top View**, add two **Empty** objects, as shown in the next image, and place them in the corners:

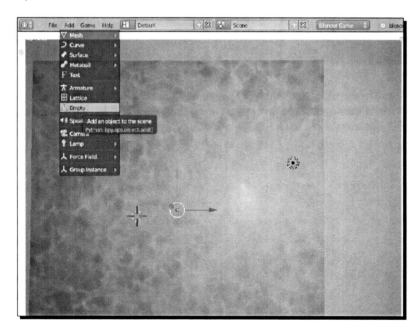

**6.** Make sure that shading is in GLSL, in the **Scene Properties** tab, or else change it. In the **Properties** tab for the object data, check the **Double side** option, if you don't want to see the underwater environment. Normals are active on the two sides of the plane. If your whale dives, you can see the same texture from outside.

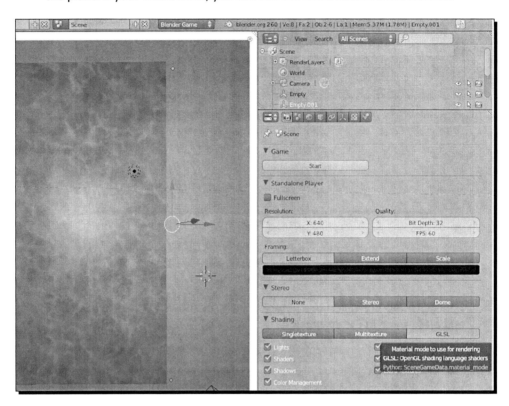

Normal maps simulate the impression of a detailed 3D surface by modifying the shading as if the surface had being completely flat. Normals indicate the direction from the face, along a line.

**7.** Insert Keyframes for each empty object and make an animation ranging from 1 to 100 frames, changing the diagonal corner position. Press the *I* key on the first frame. Go to the hundred keyframe, move the empty object to another location, and press *I* again. The animation is recorded:

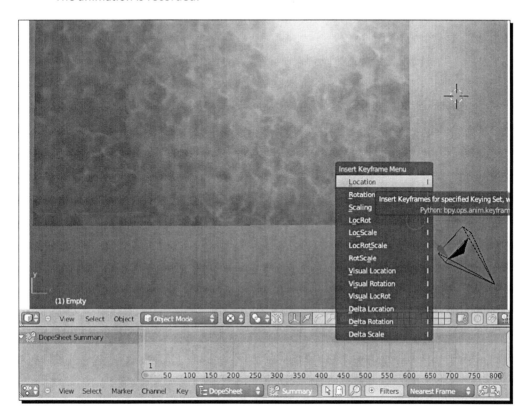

 The diagonal corner position of the empty objects are needed to move simultaneously in different directions than the water could have.

**8.** Return to the modifier's **Properties** tab, change the values in the **Textures Coordinates** for **Object**, and then select one of the empty objects, as shown in the following screenshot:

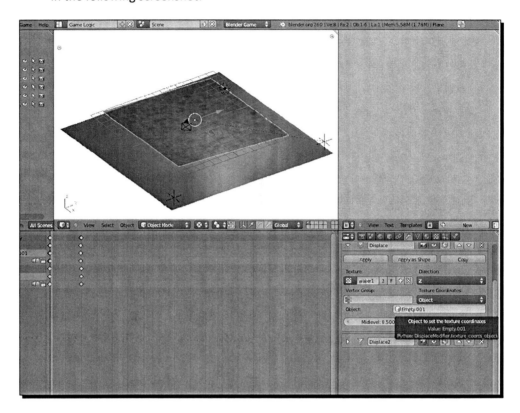

**9.** Ok, we're ready to go to **Logic Editor**. Select **Always** as the value for **Sensor**, add **And** as the value for **controller**, and at last, add **Action** as the value for **Actuator**. Connect them, as seen in the following image. Now, there are two ways that you can do the next part. They both work fine, so it just depends on your preference.

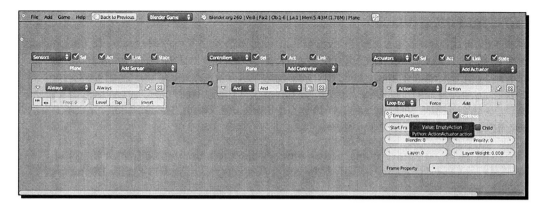

**10.** First of all, we need to change the **Action** type to **Loop End**. This will repeat the animation over and over again, and you can see it in the previous step (see the last image). The other way to do this is to leave **Action** set to **Play**, and make the sensor **True** (confirm that you press the button with three dots). See the next image with these last connections, but you can use only one of them:

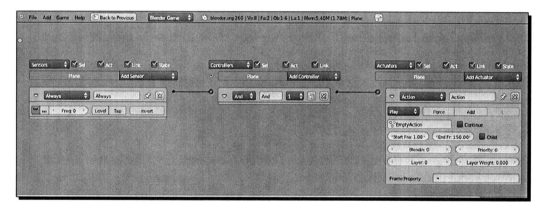

**11.** Press *P* to see the results.

## *What just happened?*

Well, I think this last one is a high-level of learning, although it was necessary to understand how to make realistic water-rendering engine. If it does not look realistic once you have checked out the results, make sure that you have not left out any of the steps performed previously. What we have done here is we have used the normal map, or texture, of a plane to move the texture without needing to move the plane. This is useful and minimizes the number of calculations in the game engine.

To be able to move normal maps, use an empty object to animate itself. After that, the normal maps need to be anchored to the empty objects, and this will enable the normal maps to move.

To create the waves, we have two empty objects to give more realism, since the water always seems to have more than one direction, but maybe it is not necessary.

## Have a go hero – making it look real

In this case, it is easy to improve the animation. Water and fluids, in general, have always been a challenge for computer calculation.

Try to make a seabed and see how it changes the look of the textures in translucent water.

You can increase the number of waves, as there are always different ways of seeing the sea, and of course, changing the color of the ocean, because in reality, it is constantly changing!

# Summary

Perhaps this chapter is the most difficult one, but you've almost reached the meridian of learning about the game engine in Blender.

Virtually everything that happens in a game has to do with what we have explained in this chapter, and it is especially related to the global virtual world simulation. Remember these steps:

1. **Restarting the position**: In every game, there is always a restart, either because you have not achieved the goal or because you have found something unexpected. This feature is essential for any type of game.

2. **Opening and closing the door**: Yes, we know, there are no doors in the Arctic, although they are extremely useful to divert the course of our character. With the **Near** function, we have seen that this is possible. With a little practice, you will find it much more useful with a single function.

3. **Natural motion**: It is impossible to understand a world without gravity. Although this was a virtual world, the objects are reacting when there are collision. This is a point where it leads us to experimentation. The physics Blender engine may leave us amazed.

4. **Making waves**: Finally, we have proved that we can cheat physics with a bit of animation and with a very special trick, moving normal maps of our water. We don't use particle simulation for water. This trick is ideal to make little the not big calculations of the game engine. Some changes in values for the same material can drastically change the results and convert water to mercury or lava.

In this chapter, we have learned to practice how objects react to the virtual world. In the next chapter, we will see how this affects the interface of the game. This covers how we can apply a level of health to our character, which level of control we need to go to, or how much money we have, and of course, if we need to change characters. Fascinating, right? Let's try it!

# 5
# Gameplay

*The part of a game that is less creative is controlled, at all times, to show the reactions of our character when it interacts with the surrounding world. It is often seen in games that form a simple interaction, for example, after a bullet hit, the character suffers a decline in its life indicator bar. Also, if we get food, weapons, or coins, depending on how the game is designed, there are indicators to show that these objects have been collected or achieved. In some games, a character can move to the other areas in the same level, and this form of interaction is necessary to show it! Or depending on the level of difficulty that we are in, we may want to change our character's viewpoint to understand better the labyrinth we are in.*

In this chapter, we will discuss the following essentials:

- ◆ Growing the character
- ◆ Creating a life indicator bar
- ◆ Creating a counter of items collected
- ◆ Creating a map of the level we play
- ◆ Changing camera views
- ◆ Moving to another level

So, let's go in steps.

# Growing the character

We know that as the game progresses (which is your character leveling), it increases the level's capabilities, weapons, and awards. The most direct way, almost always, is to make your character grow. How do we determine at what point we should start growing our character? Let's examine this.

## Time for action – counting

The counters are useful for getting some extra points, a score in the game, and certainly, it keeps a track of objects. As an example, if we get three fish, we will grow larger in size. The easiest way is to deal with the food. Let's have a look at how it will work.

We will post our whale and four icebergs. Each time you pass one of them, you add a point. When you get four points earned, you can change the look.

1. Choose **File | Append**, and select the whale. Press **Link** and **Append** from the **Library** button to add to the scene. Follow the the same step to add the four icebergs, as shown in the following screenshot:

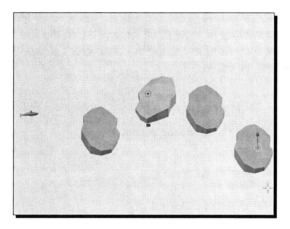

   If you see the **Append** option turned off, be sure that you are not in **Edit Mode**. In **3D View**, change to **Object Mode** or press the *Tab* button to turn on some of the items in the drop-down list.

2. Select the player with **Physics Type** as **Dynamic**, check **Actor**, and add a Game Property called `NumIcebP` for **Add Game Property** (where `NumIcebP` is the number of icebergs, and gets the value `player`):

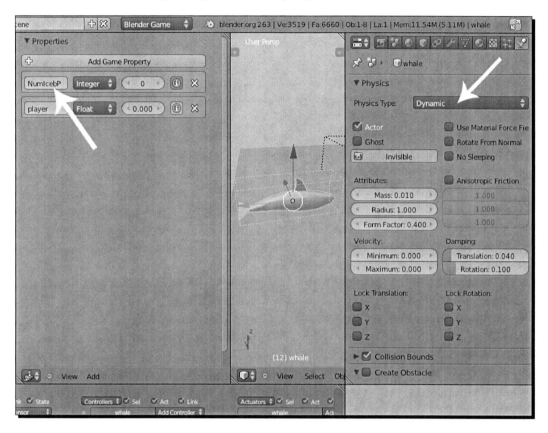

3. Select the icebergs, choose the **Physics Type** as **Dynamic**, and select **Ghost** so that the whale can pass through the iceberg, thus making the iceberg disappear. Mark the **Collision Bounds** box too.

**4.** Go to **Logic Editor**, click on **Add**, add **Touch** as the value for **Sensor** for the first iceberg, select **And** as the value for **Controller**, **Add Edit Object** as the value for **Actuator**, and choose **End Object** in the **Edit Object** drop-down list:

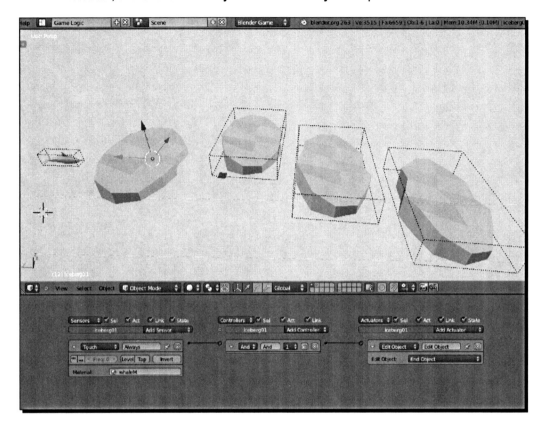

**5.** Select the whale again and **Add Touch** as the value for **Sensor**, **And** as the value for **Controller**, and **Property** as the the value for **Actuator**. In the **Property** actuator's mode, choose **Add**, select `NumIcebP` as the value for **Property** that we created, enter 1 as the value for **Value** as shown in the following screenshot, and connect the bricks:

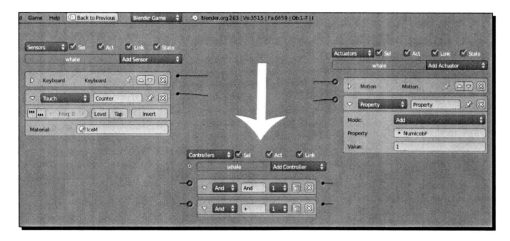

 In the **Material** option, enter the material of the icebergs as a filter for the **Touch** sensor.

**6.** If you want to see the collision between the whale in the iceberg, go to the **Game** menu, and select **Show Debug Properties**.

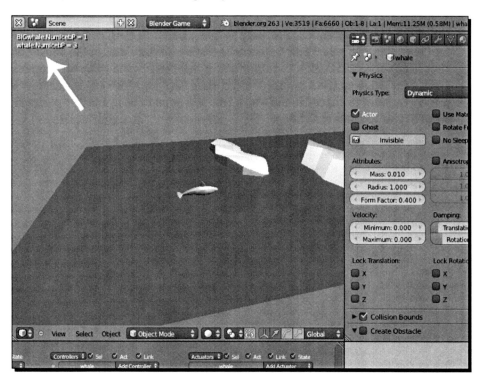

**7.** Press the *I* button of the NumIcebP property, since we can see the count/number of icebergs being displayed when we are in **Game Mode**:

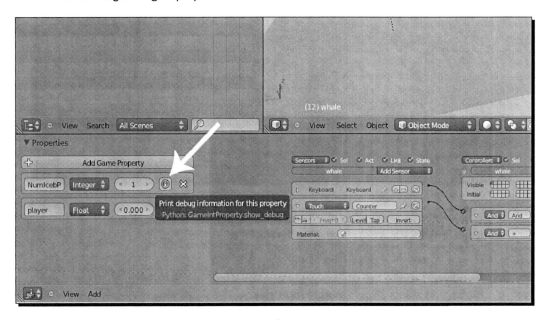

**8.** Select the player and choose **Property** as the value for **Sensor**, add **And** as the value for **Controller**, and select **Edit Object** as the value for **Actuator**. In the **Sensor** brick, choose **Equal** for **Evaluation Type**, and select NumIceP as the value for **Property**. Enter 3 for **Value**. In the **Actuator** brick, choose **Replace Mesh** and indicate which player you want to change in the **Mesh** box. You need to have a bigger player in the second layer to make the change:

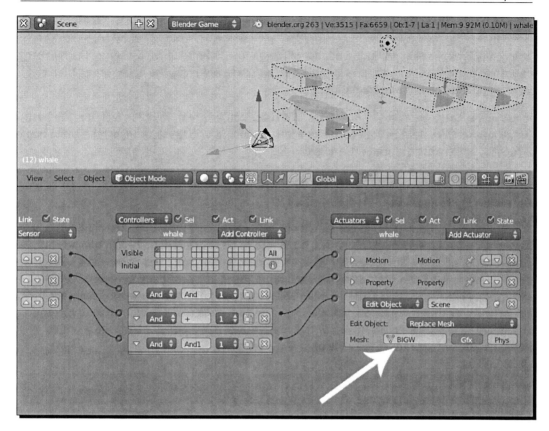

 We have duplicated the whale, scaled it up, and moved to the second layer. We have renamed it as BIGW (big whale).

## What just happened?

Thanks to the specific property of the player that we created as icebergs, we can make a change in the size of our character once the objectives have been achieved, reaching a row of objects. With the **Edit Object** option, we can assure that we have linked the actuator to replace the character with the same, but modified the player. So, what is the trick? We have prepared an identical model in another layer, but at a different scale.

## Have a go hero – completing possibilities

The ability to make changes in the middle of the game is infinite. If we recognize that we can choose to put different characters in one layer, and different weapons in the other, then can you imagine the possible combinations?

If you agree, there are many connections, but these can be great, right? In fact, it is the basis for all avatars to customize your own character. If you don't do these changes, the game does it for you, while you advance in the levels.

# Creating a life indicator bar

Surely, a game without your life bar would not be a game. One way or another, there is always a life bar present in video games. It is a rule to be respected: no health bar, no consequences (loss of life) is possible in an interactive game. Don't you believe in it? When you test a game and you can't arrive to the final, without any possibility to repeat the action instantly, the life bar has no sense. The life bar shows you how many times you have another opportunity. With this visual bar, you can improve your game and you will arrive to the end. Is the game always a way to test you or to know if you are competent? Let's see a simple demonstration of how to create a life bar.

## Time for action – decreasing life

Let's start by creating a simple life bar (two bars). Remember that the life bar is green or blue, and when you lose life the bar becomes red. Try to create a rectangle of the color you want, create another similar rectangle a bit away in the same front axis, and change its color to red.

1. Make a rectangle and duplicate it. Move to the z axis (press *Z* to snap it), and choose the color for each one, just as shown in the following screenshot:

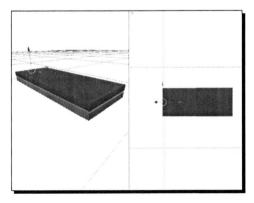

Put the cursor on the center-left edge of the rectangle, as shown in the previous screenshot.

2. Press *I* (*I* not *L*) to insert a key in the first frame, and another again in the hundredth frame, to scale the rectangle. Make the rectangle as tiny as you like in the first frame, and set it to the default rectangle shape in frame 100. See the split images in the following screenshot and observe the difference:

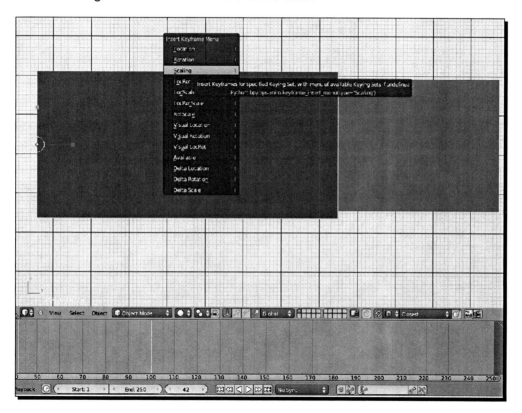

**3.** Insert it in the scene with the player (maybe a whale) and the object with which the collision occurs (a little iceberg). Remember to use **File | Append** to add the objects:

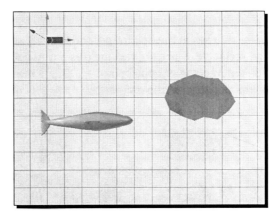

**4.** Select the whale, and press **Add Game Property** to include the property life in the whale with value `100` as **Integer**, as shown in the following screenshot:

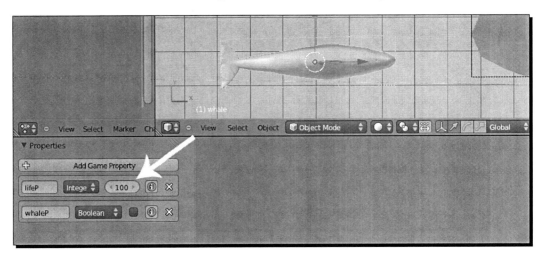

 As a solution for not getting confused between the names of objects and it's properties, you can type *P* at the end of the text, for example, `lifeP` to the property life for whale. For your character, you can decide to make a property called `whaleP` or rename it to `playerP`.

**5.** Go to the **Logic Editor** window, and add a new **Sensor** called **Collision**. Select **And** as the value for **Controller**, and select **Property** as the value for the **Actuator** that is called. Connect them and enter the values mentioned next:

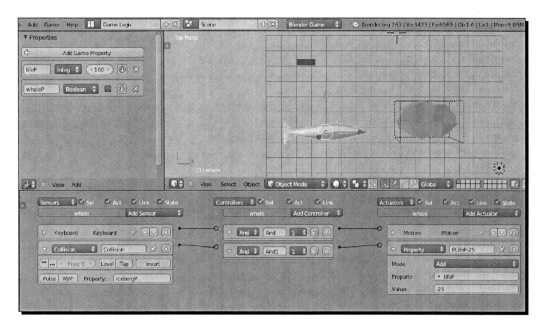

The **Actuator** property has three options. Choose **Add** in **Motion**, because you want to change the value of the whale life. Select the exact property that you want to change in the drop-down menu, in this case, `lifeP`. At last, enter the value to decrease, for example `-25`.

**6.** Select the `barlife_blue` rectangle in the 3D view. Add the next logic bricks as **Message (Sensors)**, **And (Controllers)**, and **Action (Actuators)**. Connect them after writing some input values in the blanks in **Actuators**:

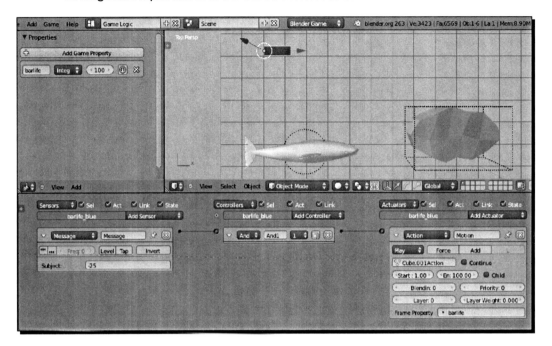

The value of **Subject** in **Message** is **-25** for the **Sensors** bricks. Only the messages with this value have effects in the connections. Choose **Play** in the **Actuator** panel, and select which motion was created in the **Dope** sheet to decrease the life bar in the drop-down list.

## What just happened?

We have inserted certain properties in the game in which we can play with variables, that is, send messages, to numerically change the properties of the objects. In our game, we changed to a lower value of our character's life when a collision occurred. If you crash, you lose some life, is it true? Here are some guidelines to do it:

◆ Create a simple life bar model

◆ Scale it in one axis with motion, inserting the change in keyframes 1 and 100

◆ Create a **Property** game called `LifeP`

- Select the player to create a collision and send a message to `barlife` with logic bricks
- Decrease `barlife` if you get a message from `player`

## Have a go hero – making limits

We have explained how to decrease the health bar due to collisions. However, wouldn't it be interesting to create a health bar yourself, wherein the health increases when your character gets food or certain objects?

I think it's a bit like thinking you will find a way to increase the life bar. Just use the same logic bricks with a positive value.

But what if you already have a full life bar, or vice versa, your life bar is empty. You will find very useful information if you said the sensor to use is **Property,** and the property chooses `Lifep` and you give a value of `0`. With this information, you can connect the bricks so that the actuator chosen in the game quits the game, or if you prefer another scene, it selects a new scene as the end of the game.

# Creating a counter of items collected

Like the life bar, we can find a counter or some objects, such as onscreen icons, to show us what we have achieved. Imagine that the whale can get floaters and these are displayed on screen. Let's see how to get it.

## Time for action – collecting

The process is always the same: we have a collision in order to prove that the player really has got the medal, trophy, or in our case, the iceberg. To do this, we must create a collision after appending the whale in our new scene by performing the following steps:

1. Choose **File | Append**, and select the iceberg file to get the object. Move it to get to the front of our player to make a collision, and duplicate it two times. Scale them as icons, and reposition them to the right-top screen corner:

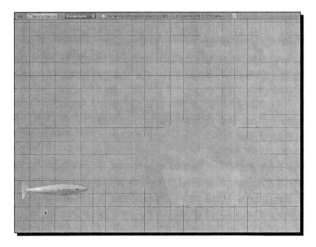

2. Create a game object attribute called `icebergP` in the **Game Properties** section as an **Integer** with value 2, as shown in the following screenshot (we have two icebergs as icons and you can see that we just created a **Keyboard** sensor to move the whale):

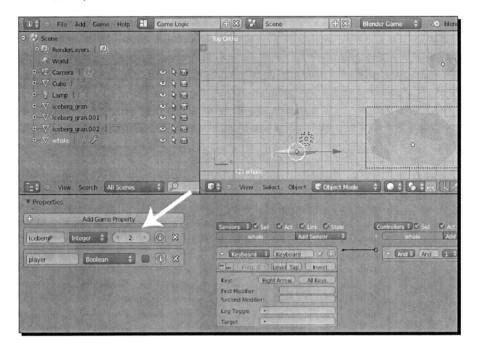

Select the whale before adding `icebergP` object properties. Each collision of the whale will remove an iceberg icon on the screen.

3.  We need an answer when the whale has a collision. In this case, we need two answers at the same time. We need to change the value of **Property** to `icebergP` when the collision occurs, and send a message to the iceberg icon to hide it. For that, select **Add Collision** as the value for **Sensor**, **Add And** as the value for **Controller**, and **Property** as the value for **Actuator** in **Logic Editor**. Fill in the blanks of **Actuator** as shown in the following screenshot, selecting the **Add** option in **Mode**, `icebergP` as a property to change, and `-1` as **Value** to change:

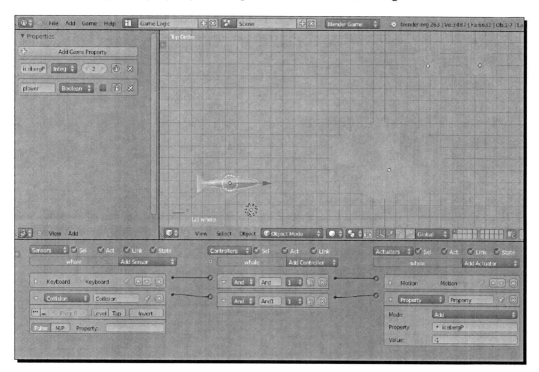

 All connections that we need are not complete. Follow step 4 and then read step 5 back-to-back and finish the necessary connections of our player.

**4.** If the collision must change the value of the properties of the icebergs, we need to show how to indicate that on our screen. We need to hide one iceberg icon. Select the last iceberg icon and make these connections. Add **Message** as the value for **Sensor**, add **And** as the value for **Controller**, and add **Edit Object** as the value for **Actuator**. The result is to hide the iceberg icon when we choose the **End** object.

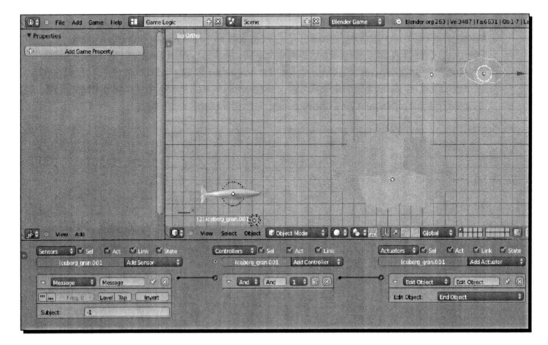

 The iceberg icon lasts only until it receives a message with the exact value.

5. The message sends the confirmation that the collision has been made, and at the same time, shows you a tiny iceberg as a counter and how many icebergs you have left. Add a **Message** actuator and choose the object to send the message by selecting it in the blank space. Type -1 in the cell subject. Make the connection as shown in the following screenshot:

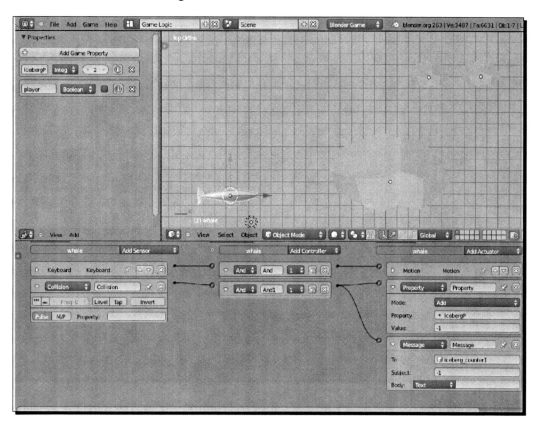

**6.** If there are no iceberg icons in the game, we can change the scene to the next level. Add **Property** as the value for **Sensor**, add **And** as the value for **Controller**, and add **Scene** as the value for **Actuator**. Choose the next scene that you created.

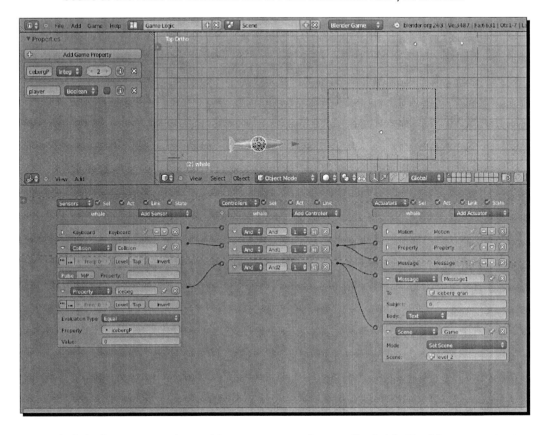

We again linked two connections with one sensor and controller brick. The **Message** actuator is the same one that was created in the last step, changing the values shown to you in the image before. Create a new **Actuator** called **scene**, but make a new one in the 3D view before choosing them in **Logic Bricks.** It is necessary to have another scene before we make the bricks.

## What just happened?

Collecting objects is a common practice at all levels of play. To show how it is progressing, everything is set, to send and receive messages to the variables we created, so that each object has its properties. This is how we have done it:

◆ Making an icon object to show on the screen

◆ Creating a game property in our player to count the icons with a numeric value

- ◆ Selecting the player to perform a collision and changing the numeric value
- ◆ Showing or hiding the counters on receiving a message of collision of the player
- ◆ Selecting the player to send a message to the icons with logic bricks
- ◆ Checking if the icons are complete, and changing the level of the game

We performed a simple test object reduction, although the steps are the same for more life, other weapons, and of course, the coins of Mario Bros!

## Have a go hero – making the difference

Once we have understood that the message is necessary to send values and determine the calculation to show or hide icon bars, you can consistently achieve an advanced level of counters. If you get a full blue counter, for example, then you can get a green one, making you bigger, stronger, or something else. Many strategy games are based only on these icons, and should have them under control. These icons should not fill the screen. When the screen is full, it creates inconvenience by affecting the visibility for the player. The icons must match the type of game and should minimize distractions.

A very common practice is to perform a double life bar. If our character obtains an armor or shield, you could use a second life bar to extend the character's ability to fight. Try it! It is very interesting.

Maybe your type of game is not collecting items. However, you can translate the way you do it if you want to make a timer, a save point, or save stats for the player on his corner of the configuration screen.

# Creating a map of the level we play

A game is not complete if we cannot show the map of the level we're playing in. In *Chapter 3, The First Level*, we mentioned that the map design was the most important part. Now is time to learn it.

## Time for action – overlaying something like a map

This technique is applicable to maps and anything that we want to be superimposed on our screen as a **Heads-up Display (HUD)** . Imagine a whale hunter as a sniper: if we press an *S* key that implies we have superimposed crosshairs. We will see the scene with a crosshair in the middle as a hunter with his weapon. In the same way, if we press the *M* key, we should see an overlaid map in the scene. Let's try it first.

1. Make a new scene, rename it as CROSSMAP, and add a camera at a position, as shown in the following screenshot:

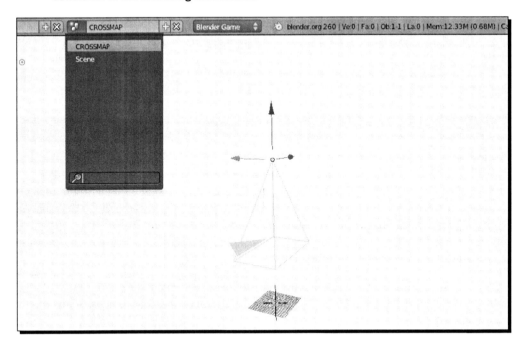

2. Press *0* (camera view) and add a map of your level in a PNG format. Scale it and reposition it in the left-bottom corner. In this case, we are modeling a cross, but it can be substituted for anything that you want to see in the screen of the player.

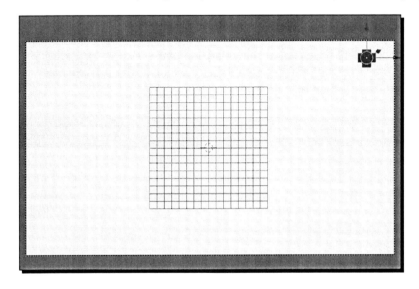

If you put a camera on top of your level, you can save it as an image in a PNG format of your map level of the game, and use it for this new scene.

3. Go back to the scene of the game level and select the principal camera. Go to **Logic Editor**. Add **Always** as the value for **Sensors**, add **And** as the value for **Controllers**, and add **Scene** as the value for **Actuators**. In type of **Scene**, choose **Add Overlay Scene**, and then select CROSSMAP (or the scene that you want). Make the connections:

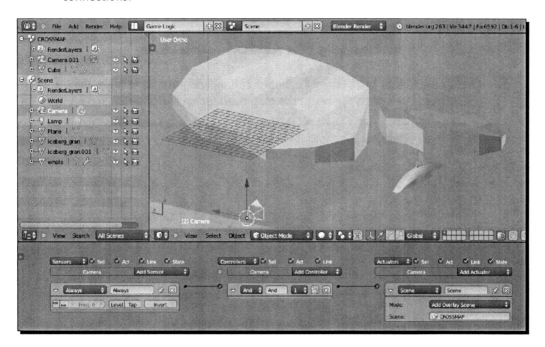

4.  Press *P* to see the results. The scene is always overlay, and we need to show and hide the map (icon) information. Let's change it.

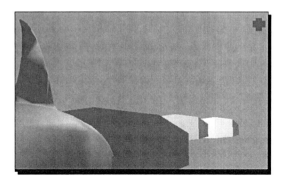

5.  Change the **Sensor** brick to the **Keyboard** option, and press *M* to make the connection. Even press the key in the map overlapping the screen:

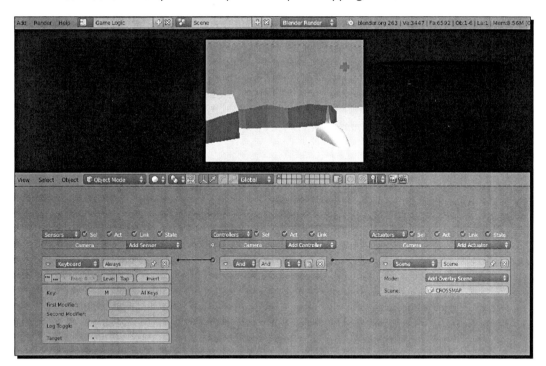

**6.** Set the same connection if you want to remove the overlay scene, as shown in the following screenshot:

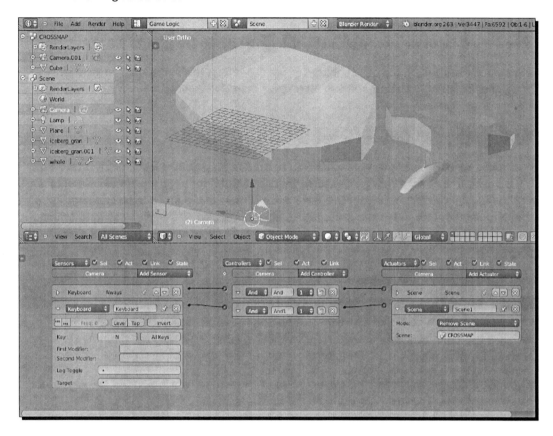

## What just happened?

We have learned to connect and overlay several scenes at the same time, from a sensor provided as a **Keyboard** sensor. We started out with a second scene to set the camera, as well as overlapping the object you want to view. Then, we returned to the main scene in the game to connect the logic brick for the actuator. This makes the scene appear onscreen to show the HUD.

**Have a go hero – remaking things**

Well, we are clear about what a HUD needs to go through in an actuator with overlay. So, to modify every scene and set the bar of life, potential counters, map, and so on, you can think of new situations or scenarios that enable them to be shown or hidden in the main scene.

If we place a red ball on top of our character, we can reflect this in the map on a smaller scale, thus changing a static map to an interactive map. Are you ready to do it yourself?

# Changing the camera view

Practically, we use a single camera when you're used to playing on a level, but it is true that if it is possible to change views it can sometimes be helpful for us to do. In the case of racing or shooting, it is almost necessary to have a point of view in the first person and another in the third person. This makes the gameplay change drastically. Finally, we're used to seeing another camera (point of view) with a very open view to show more of the levels we're playing in.

**Time for action – view 1, 2, 3**

Once you learn how to assign a camera to a point of view, all of the other cameras are assigned the same way. Yet, it's important to know in what order to place them there, and what kind of plane we use for each of them.

If you use a descending order, the player can easily remember which number key is used for each type of view. The following example demonstrates this:

1. Let's use our character in the Arctic to place three cameras. The scene must have the whale and some icebergs. Add the cameras, and be sure to rename the cameras as `camera1` (first person), `camera2` (third person), and `camera3` (Open view), as seen in the following screenshot. Change the location and rotation of all of them wherever you need.

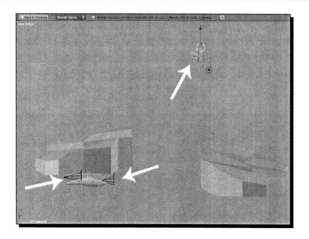

 Scale the cameras to see them better. Scaling it does not affect the proportions, it only makes them visible. Use two 3D monitor views for positioning the cameras well. Check **Clip end value** in **Properties**, if you can't see the objects that are far.

2. Let's go to **Logic Editor**, add **Keyboard** as the value for **Sensors**, add **And** as the value for **Controllers**, and add **Scene** as the value for **Actuators**. Choose **Set Camera** in the **Scene** option, and select the correct camera in **Camera Object** of the actuator that you have selected. Repeat the process for two more cameras:

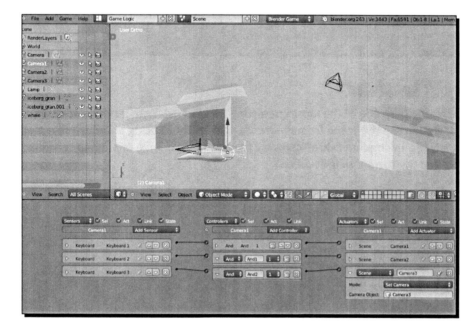

**3.** Select one camera for a last connection. You need the cameras to follow the player and not to see how it crosses in front of it. Add **Always** as the value for **Sensors**, **And** as the value for **Controllers**, and **Camera** as the value for **Actuators**. Select the player in the camera object, and make the brick connections. Press *P* to see the results:

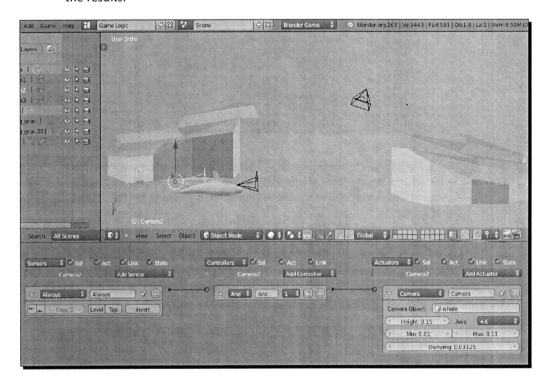

## What just happened?

We have finally seen one of the most interesting tricks of 3D. With a simple addition of more cameras, we can see the scene from different angles without being afraid of movement errors. Placing a minimum of three cameras provides a view large enough to see your character and the surrounding scenery.

Thanks to the easy use of logic bricks with keys 1, 2, and 3, we have connected the keyboard numbers to each of the cameras located on our stage. In order for the camera to follow the player, we have seen how the object connects and that selecting this is possible.

## Have a go hero – not the only point of view

The cameras have a particular purpose, disposing them off at all times is not a good use of resources for the game. Therefore, you should not always have the same camera for all of the levels.

If your game was a race car, it would obviously need the camera for the mirror, right? Use the technique learned here to improve situations. You need to use new positions of the cameras to increase the gameplay. If your game is about a war, would you not need a camera that uses a sniper effect?

There are always interesting views. Remember, we have not touched the camera settings, and you can always change their properties so that each one has more differences, and are not only the point of view.

# Moving to another layer

Imagine that our level of play has a lot of objects around, and we do not want to fill the main stage with them. A good practice would be to think that it is better to remove the objects that are not required, so as to not have any unnecessary performance in the same scene.

# Time for action – throwing things

If you need to shoot or throw objects, you need to launch projectiles constantly. We don't need to place the exact number of bullets for the same number of objects to be destroyed in the scene, without knowing how many bullets our player gets to use. Here is a sample.

*1.* To throw an object in the game engine, we will work in two different layers. In the first one, we are going to put an empty object. In the second one, we will put the object to be released. Go to **Menu** and choose **Add | Empty**:

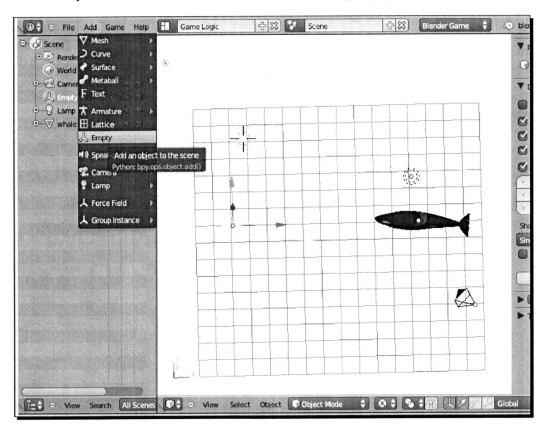

**2.** We select the second layer (shown in red) and create a harpoon that will be our missile. To be safe and to avoid any mistakes, you're going to put a name. Press *N*, and add the name `harpoon`:

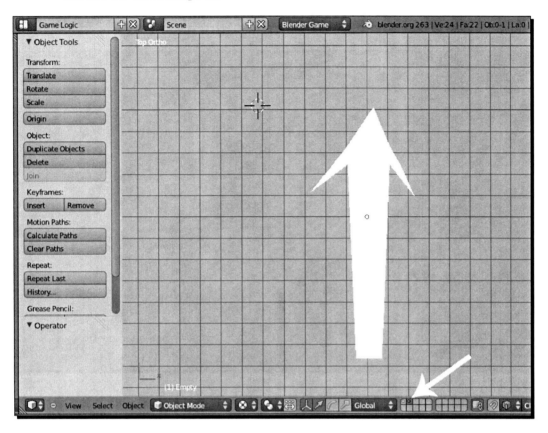

3. Go to **Logic Editor**, and choose **Always** as the value for **Sensors**, **And** as the value for **Controllers**, and **Motion** as the value for **Actuators**, to move the harpoon. Type the exact value of the coordinates of the harpoon that you want to move it to. Finally, add **Collision** as the value for **Sensors**, **And** as the value for **Controllers**, and **Edit Object** as the value for **Actuators**, with **End Object** type to finally connect the bricks:

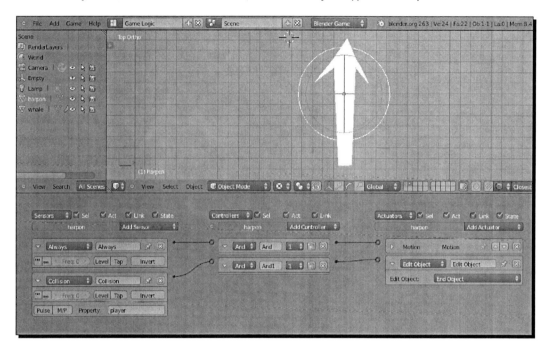

4. Go back to the first layer and click on **Logic Editor**. Add **Always** as the value for **Sensors**, **And** as the value for **Controllers**, and **Edit Object** as the value for **Actuators**, with **Add Object** type. Connect the bricks and press *P*:

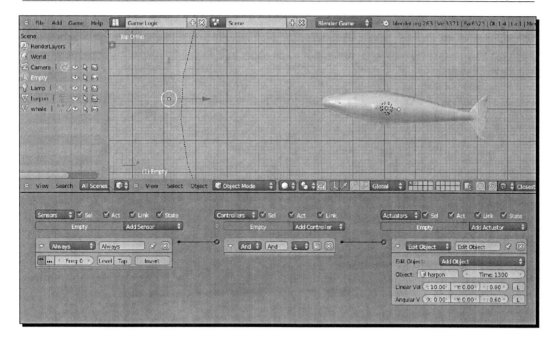

## What just happened?

Layers allow you to store the objects that somehow are not required in the main scene, at least not all of the time, as the main character is . To do this, we have placed a child object as a harpoon into a second layer with a constant speed of action.

We have called the object of the second layer from the main layer, thanks to the **Empty** objects located in the scene. This resource may be used as many times as necessary. The most illustrative example of all is to understand the use of an **Empty** object as the ammunition.

## Have a go hero – making the shooter

A good exercise would be to modify the **Keyboard** sensor by tightening a button, so that you can shoot as much as you want. Remember, you can modify the properties of the object and make any shot look more realistic. Adding a blur effect can be interesting, and looking through the options of the **2D Filter** actuator may surprise you more than once.

## Pop quiz – moving to another level

Perhaps this chapter is a bit repetitive, but each topic has a specific role with bricks that was worth exploring.

1. Which type of **Edit Object** actuator needs to delete an object in your scene?

   a. Replace Mesh

   b. Add Object

   c. End Object

2. To make some variables in the game, you must include which of the following?

   a. A game property

   b. A sensor property

   c. A property actuator

3. To send and receive messages, you will need which of the following?

   a. Message Sensor

   b. Receive Actuator

   c. Both

# Summary

We have already reached the end of the chapter. Let's review everything we've seen.

We have learned to switch between the characters within the game. It can also be applied to modify any object within the level. We have seen that through collisions, we can create a life bar that increases or decreases according to the player's decisions. Also, we have seen that certain properties of the object can count and number certain actions before passing the level. It is a good method to test the reflexes of the player.

We picked up a lesson covered in *Chapter 3*, *First Level*, and we're done with the secret of maps, and adding more than one scene of the game at the moment. We can finally find some points of view cameras, as well as change the gameplay.

Finally, we have taken the game to another level, discovering how to automate certain actions of the player, as simple as shooting or throwing missiles.

It's now time to move on to the next chapter, where we will meet again.

# 6
# Liven up Your World!

*We have a very clear idea of our character, but the specifics may be an area of concern. We need to be clear about the specifics from the beginning if we want to improve our game with minor changes. You will agree when I say that it is not the same as seeing your character fall or perform a roll on the floor if it collides with any object. It is the same with the process of walking, sitting, bending, and so on. All of these possibilities are small changes in our character, but it makes it extremely important to bring our game to life.*

In this chapter we will see how to:

◆ Animate the character

◆ Make the environment come alive

◆ Animate your enemies

◆ Make your own game

So let's get started.

## Animate the character

Having a list of all of the actions we need for our character will help us later to create some animations, including connecting all of them to seem even more fluid. If your character walks, runs, stands, sits, or skips, any of these things must be in tune with the last move we have on display. We can create some small animations for them that summarize the most commonly used options.

# Time for action – moving the whale's tail

There are many manuals on how to create skeletons for our characters. However, we present a basic example that you yourself must develop further, with better complexity, for each type of character you need to model. In this case, we will move our whale's tail, which is translated to the axis rotated in the y value.

**1.** Click on **Add | Armature | Single Bone** to start building the skeleton of the whale:

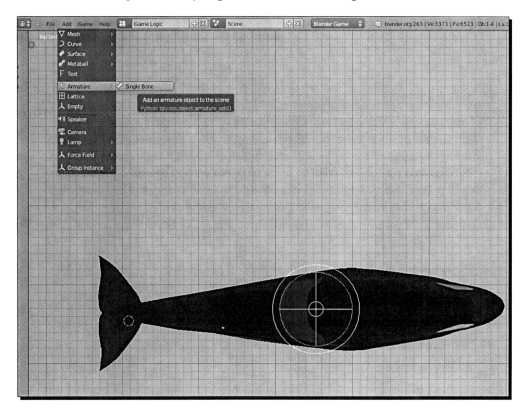

Select **Edit Mode** to click on the last joint and press *E* to add another joint. Another way to do this is to go to the **3D View** menu and select **Armature | Extrude**.

2. To attach the object to the armature, switch to **Object Mode,** select the object and then the armature with the *Shift* key pressed. Then parent it to the armature by pressing the key combination *Ctrl + P,* and then select the **With Automatic Weights** option in **Armature Deform**:

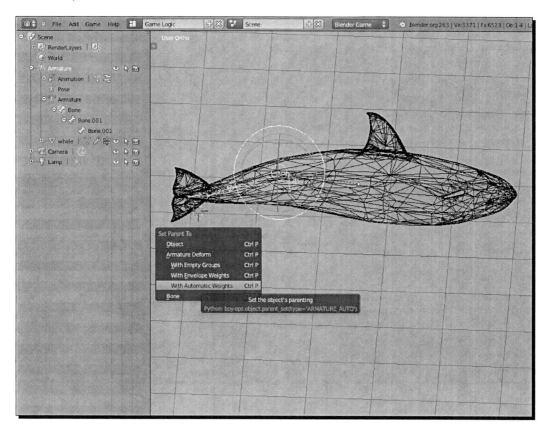

The other method to parent objects is by using the built-in option in the **3D View** menu bar. For this, switch to **Object Mode** and first select the object and then the armature or bones with the *Shift* key pressed. Then go to the **3D View** menu bar and select **Object | Parent | Set | Armature Deform | With Automatic Weights**.

**3.** Switch to **Pose Mode**, and press *I* to insert a keyframe and select the
**Rotation** option:

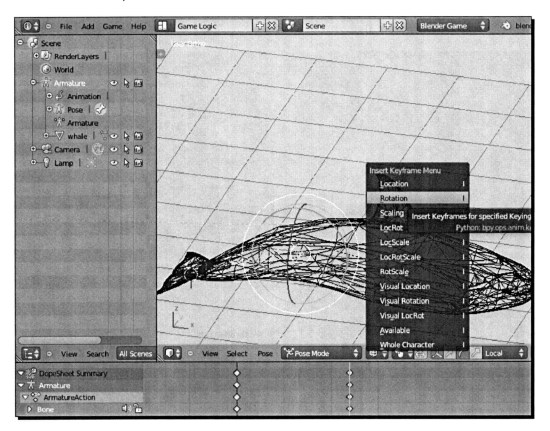

 If you want to see the **NLA Editor** (Non-Linear Animation), display it in a split
screen to see the keyframes inserted.

**4.** Move the Timeline's green bar in the **NLA Editor** to frame 15, rotate the bone a little bit more down and press *I* to insert other keyframe. Do the same to frame 30. You have made your first animation on the tail of the whale:

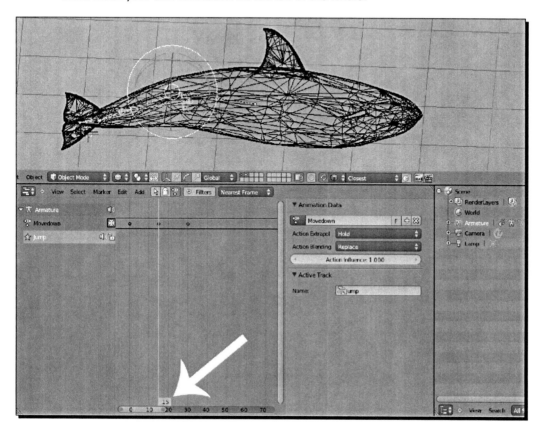

 Press *N* in the **NLA Editor** type and change the name of your armature animation in the ID name section as **Movedown**.

**5.** If you want to add more short animations, press the + button to create new actions and modify the rotations of your ends bones. Press the **DopeSheet** button to browse the action to be linked, as shown in the next screenshot:

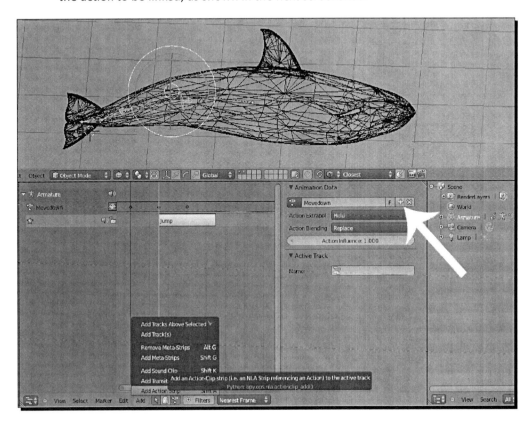

**6.** Go to **Logic Editor** and create a **Keyboard** sensor, **And** controller, and two actuator bricks: a **Motion** actuator to move our whale in the scene and an **Action** actuator for selecting which animation you want. Connect them as shown in the next screenshot:

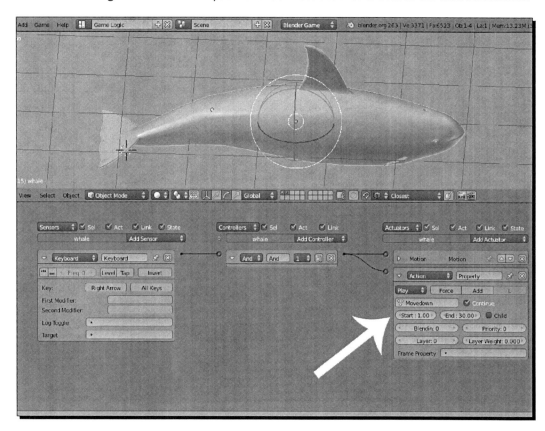

 Remember, you must write the **Start** and **End** of frames in the **Action** brick panel.

**7.** Connect the rest of the **Action** bricks with their own **Motion** as shown in the next screenshot:

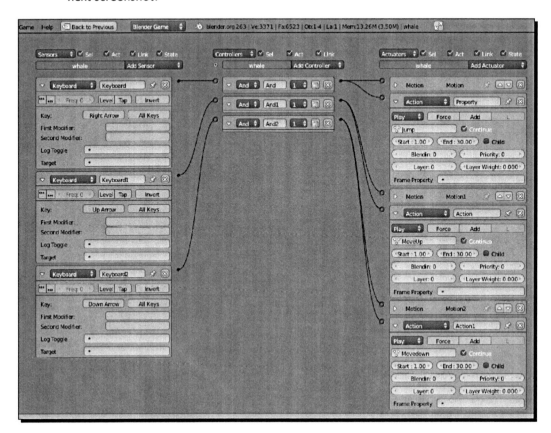

 An observation: you can see that every **Motion** has an **Action**.

# What just happened?

We have seen that each character's movement with the keyboard needed a specific action. If we pressed forward, we needed the action of walking. Similarly, if you want to make the character run, we need to take an appropriate action. Each key should take some action to make the game much more fluid.

We had to start by creating a skeleton for your character, so that once related to the mesh, the bones that make the sheet of the mesh can be rotated without needing to touch the vertex of the object.

Each rotation of the bone can be engraved with a keyframe, creating poses at the beginning and at the end of each action. NLA is responsible for creating the intermediate animation keyframes. You don't need to create the entire movement.

Once we have determined the triggers that are useful to move the character, we have **Logic Editor** to create the connections between the key on the keyboard and the character's movement, thereby performing the animation.

## Have a go hero – making poses

It is logical to tell you that you need to create many actions. No matter how small the gesture is, they make the game much more attractive. For example, opening a door, sitting, waiting with the character's head down, sitting back, and so on.

You may not need to move a character, only a certain part that greatly facilitates the work. To be fair and consistent with the beginning of this chapter, do not be distracted with trivialities, the basic options must exist. Walking, running, jumping, falling, or dying is much more necessary than the others. If they are refined, create other actions. However, do not start with the details if you do not have good main basic actions.

A character becomes a hero by creating actions that are the sum of two or more actions that will successfully create a third action. An example would be a special key that could give a super jump, bringing together the normal jump over a pirouette with a perfect fall. Do you know what I'm talking about?

# Making the environment come alive

We can play a game with no sound, but it is crucial to close certain circles of action. For example, the shot of a pistol is not the same without a sound, the car races do not have the same emotion if we do not hear the roar of the engines, and if our main character does not emit any sound when you break something, when it sets aside a tree branch, or jumps from a great height, something seems amiss. Logic bricks have a rather simple enough solution, let's see it.

## Time for action – creating sounds and music

If we could start our game by creating a library of objects, we must do the same for sounds and music. Once we make the connection to one, the rest is in the same way. So, let's start with something easy, the complexity of the sounds only depends on how good your library is.

**1.** Let's use the Internet to get our sounds. In this case, we use `http:// www. freesound.org`. Enter `whale` in the search box and choose the third option, which is **whale.wav**, to download, as shown in the following screenshot:

 You need to be logged in to download the audio tracks.

**2.** Make the connection by adding an actuator called **Sounds** and search for the audio file in the library of your PC. In our case, we use the **Up Arrow** key sensor as shown in the next screenshot to hear the sound:

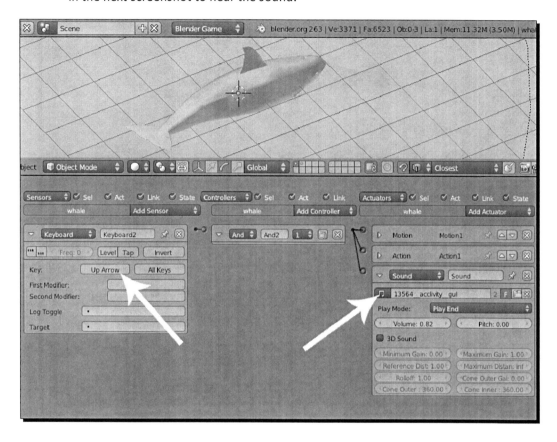

3. Select a sound from the list, or load a new one, when you press the **Open** button. Choose the audio file and select the type of **Play Mode**, for example, if you put **Play Stop**, the sound will play while you have the key pressed, and stop when you release the key:

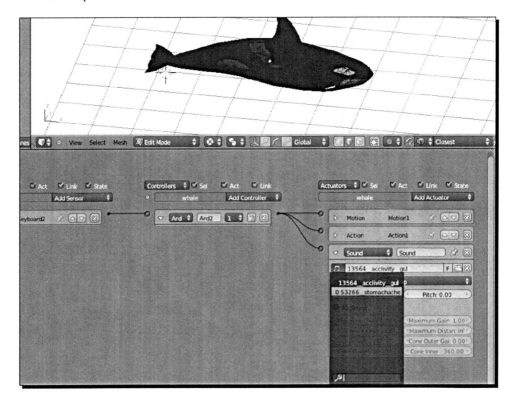

4. Choose the property panels to check the values of the sound that you believe have the best options, as shown in the next screenshot:

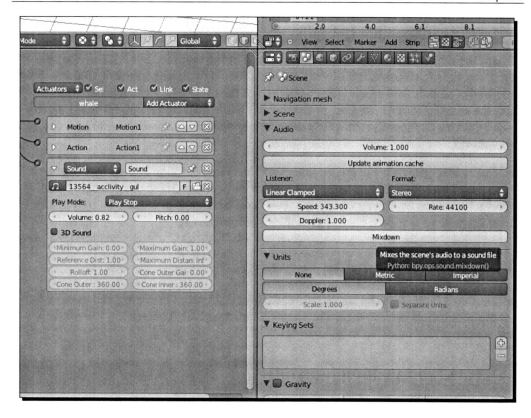

 A good practice is to use the **Format** as **Stereo** with a **44100** KHz **Rate**.

# What just happened?

We needed to collect some audio files to create our sound library. We used the Internet to demonstrate how to go about getting our audio files.

We wanted to provide certain sounds for the movements of the character, so we used the **Sound** actuator to be connected to any sensor.

First, we loaded a scene where we had set an upward movement of the whale and we took that same connection to add the **Sound** actuator, indicating that the sound file has to be played when you press the **Up Arrow** key.

## Have a go hero – sounds like music

Perhaps the main character is relevant in almost all of the chapters, but it is true that the sound was almost left aside. It is obvious that you should dedicate some time to think about what kind of sounds flow around the character, not the other way around (which would make the character sound like God, or that he was a one-man orchestra). Let the character be quiet, with a few sounds that will fill the auditory environment and almost seem like a soundtrack.

Remember that music fills the empty spaces and increases emotion in their sore spots. Create your own sound list and use it in the game without disturbing the gameplay. Each **Sound** actuator has its own audio volume level. Take advantage of options offered by the **Sound** actuator so that each file has its well-defined properties.

# Animate your enemies

There comes a time when the character needs to interact with the enemy, and as our whale cannot shoot bullets, we can make our enemy interact with our character. If the whale is near, we can get a whale ship to go hunting.

## Time for action – animating the hunter

We have learned to animate our character, so we are able to encourage our enemy by creating a simple route to the left and right, like a sentinel on the lookout. If the whale is too close to be seen, we can create a random pursuit until the whale submerges.

***1.*** Create a scene similar to the one shown in the following screenshot, with a whale, a ship, and two icebergs. Select the ship and set an action moving the ship in the x axis to different values. Insert a keyframe on frame 0, and insert another keyframe on frame 100 with another position.

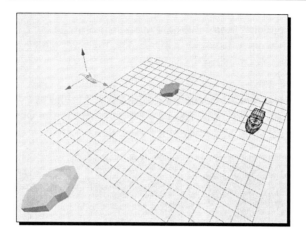

**2.** Go to **Logic Editor** and select the ship. Add the **Always** sensor, **And** controller, and **Action** actuator. Select **Action Type** as **Loop End** to repeat the action constantly, and choose which action you want for the ship:

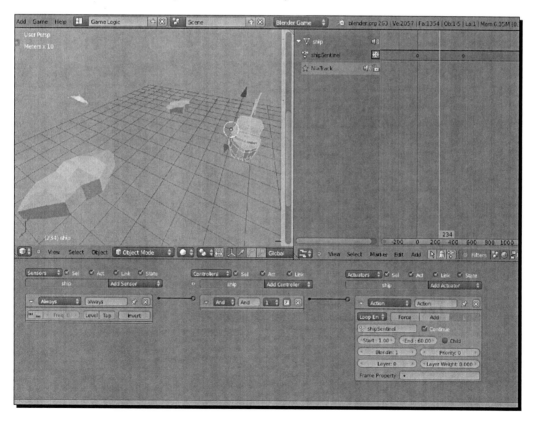

**Priority** option is used if there are many actions at the same time, and it helps to decide which is the first one. With the **Layer** option, you can make more than one action at the same time.

3. We need the **Near** sensor to apply a persecution. In this case, the **Edit Object** actuator has the option set to **Track to**. Select **whale** in the **Object** box, as shown in the next screenshot, and make the connections:

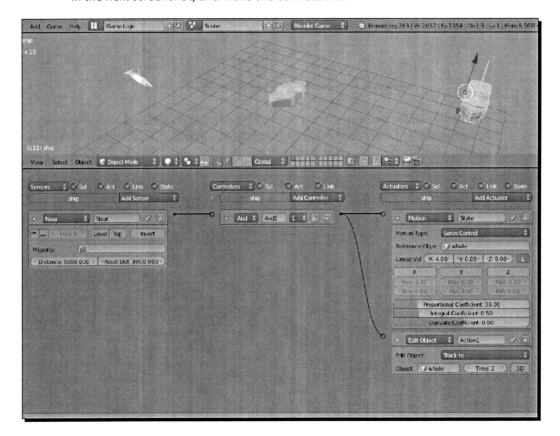

 To move the ship, we need a **Motion** actuator with a constant value. In this case, we change **Linear Vel** (linear velocity) in **X** by **4**.

## *What just happened?*

We needed to create an interaction of the enemy with the character. So we had created a constant action, which makes the boat do a patrol. Once we created the loop of the action, we had to force a proximity detector sensor with **Near**.

In this case, the sensor forced us to create two new actuators. First, the **Edit Object** of the ship with the function **Track to** to continue to follow the whale. Second, a small acceleration using **Motion,** so that it looks like the pursuit is taking speed.

## Have a go hero – kill them all

The whale cannot shoot, but it can escape under water. We cannot try to eliminate the pursuit unless the whale is further away from the boat.

You'll need to create some major collisions, which is why we have placed two icebergs on the scene. You will need to decide whether the whale, like the boat, should have consequences if they collide. Do you dare to change the status of each of them? The enemy boat, for example, could sink. Umm... I've already created an animation that you should register as an action for the boat. It never ends, right?

# Make your own game

Well, we now have the great opportunity to create our own game, but how do we do it if we have not learned to shoot. True, the whales do not shoot, so if you allow me, we make a parenthesis to explain how easy it is to add a gun to our player, our enemy, or whomever.

# Time for action – making the hunter shoot

We could not leave the explanation of how to create a shooter game, so to learn this technique, you only need to understand that a bullet is an object that appears and disappears in our level of play every time we press the trigger button. So, we must create a way for the bullet to be fired as many times as necessary, and as often as we press the firing button. If we don't shoot, we have no bullet, if we fired, there are enough bullets.

*1.* Add an empty object near the ship in the scene with some objects, as shown in the next screenshot:

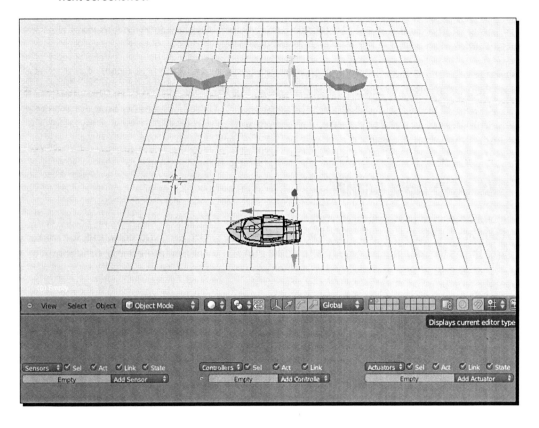

**2.** Press *Shift* and select the empty object and then the boat. Set the order of the boat to parent with *Ctrl+P*. Each time you move the boat, the empty object will follow the boat:

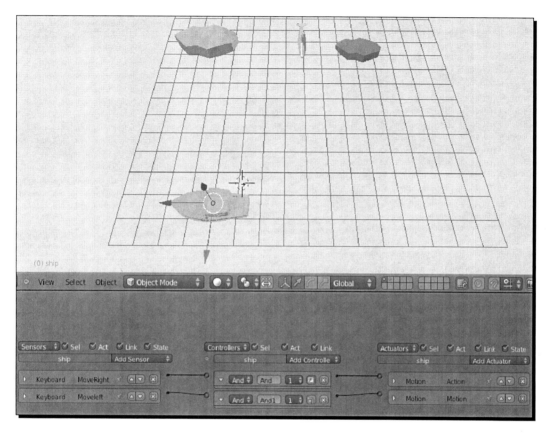

(0) ship

View   Select   Object   Object Mode   Global

Sensors   Sel   Act   Link   State          Controllers   Sel   Act   Link          Actuators   Sel   Act   Link   State
      ship          Add Sensor                      ship          Add Controlle                      ship          Add Actuator

Keyboard   MoveRight                    And   And   1          Motion   Action
Keyboard   MoveLeft                     And   And1   1          Motion   Motion

The ship has connections with two movements: left and right in the x axis.

**3.** To add a bullet, for our purpose we put on a new layer, so each time we need it, we have the bullet. Select a new layer (shown in red) and add a new cube. Stretch it into a rectangle. Rename it as `Bullet`:

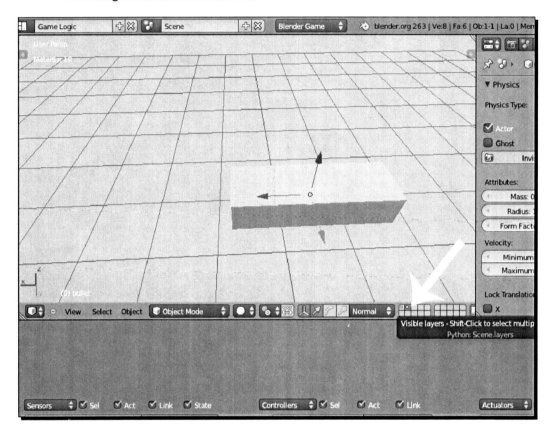

**4.** Push Layer 1 and select the empty object. Choose **Keyboard** as the sensor (**Spacebar**), add **And** as the controller, and add **Edit Object** as the actuator. In the menu, select **Bullet** as the object to be added into the scene. Connect the logic bricks as shown in the next screenshot:

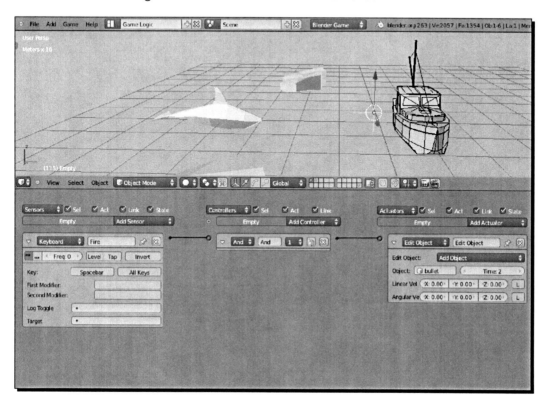

**5.** Switch to Layer 2 and select the bullet. Add **Always** as the sensor, add **And** as the controller, and **Motion** as the actuator. Change the **X** value to **5,** or any other value (depends on you) as shown in the next screenshot. Connect them. Select Layer 1 and press *P* to see the result.

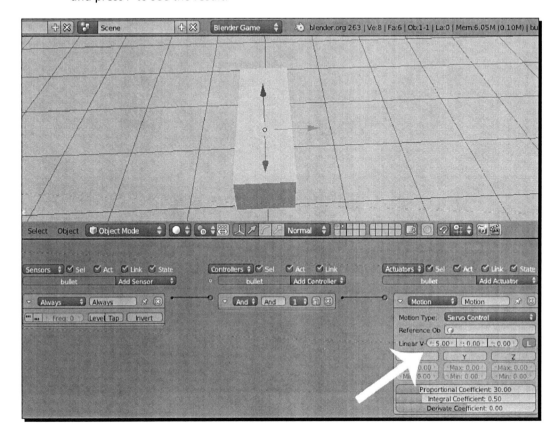

## What just happened?

We have already seen how to create the appearance of objects and interaction with our character. The common factor in many games is to give the character weapons and bullets to shoot, so we have learned through a second layer that we can add a constant object to our main stage such as a bullet in a shooter game.

We inserted an empty object in our scene, which we have related to the character or main enemy. We switched layers to model a prototype bullet with a simple cube having a constant movement in one axis. Finally, we built the logic bricks that act every time you press the space bar.

## Have a go hero – destroying things

Do not stop during this amazing exercise, continue to apply certain changes to the new objects you include in the scene. For example, it is necessary that the bullets collide with the objects. Why not try to collide these bullets with the objects in the scene? Remember, the objects may be rigid bodies, but your bullet must have dynamics for the collision to have its desired effect.

Be amazed when objects are moved by the bullet. You've built your first shooter!

## Pop quiz – make your own game

It's time for a short questionnaire:

1. If you want to change the poses of your character, which actuator do you need?

    a. Motion

    b. Action

    c. Edit object

2. Which Play mode is needed to control sound?

    a. Play End

    b. Play Stop

    c. Loop Bidirectional

3. Remember that you can change the character, skin, or add weapon to the player. Which is the actuator that you need to use to do this?

    a. Edit Object

    b. Action

    c. Property

# Summary

We could say that in this chapter, the key concept is how to liven up the game environment. Let's go step by step and remember the key tips:

♦ Creating multiple-character animations allow us to interact more efficiently with the keyboard and its functions, making the game more attractive. Taking various poses, we make the player much more versatile with its surroundings.

♦ The same thing happens to everything that we hear in our scene. It is greatly enriched if we support it with audio for good measure. Many effects and sounds are not suitable, so look for a middle and an end to strengthen it with music.

♦ If we were able to create certain poses for your character, we can do the same for our enemies by creating animations that interact in a different way if we are close. This will give the game a rhythm and will increase the tension in the gameplay.

♦ If we move, and if they move, and the life above our environment do too, we only need to destroy it. Maybe a shooter is the closest thing to sum up the essence of chaos. Delete it all, there will be nothing after you.

Oops! Sorry, we lack one important thing, the credits. Let's examine them in the next chapter.

# 7
# Game Menu Screens

*In this brief chapter, we will cover the beginning of a game, how to create menus to start playing, and how to create the executable to start the game.*

*Each game has a splash screen for the player to wait and decide whether to start, see different game parameters, and/or change the game settings by pressing the relevant buttons. You can do all this and much more. The changes are easy, and you just need to think about what you have not done before.*

Need a guide? You will surely have one as we cover the following topics:

- Making titles
- Creating simple buttons
- Making an external executable game

So let's go reading.

## Making titles

You must present the title of the game with something spectacular, or rather with something that catches your eye. Often, this title serves as the same title for the cover of many things, and is the emblem that accompanies the game during its shelf life. As time goes on, you may not remember the title, but you will never forget a cool cover, right?

## Time for action – creating your first game title

There are many ways to start a game, such as creating a picture, making a spectacular title, and so on. As an example, we can join the home screen and place two single texts. In this example, we will add a title for the game and assign a key from the keyboard that you will press to start playing.

*1.* Press **View | Top** in the 3D view, choose **Scene** in **Menu**, press the **+** button, and select **New** to add a new scene, then rename it as Maintitle:

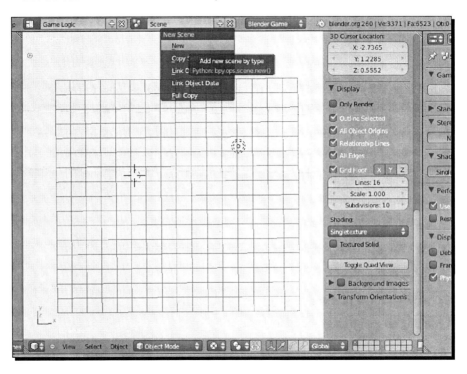

**2.** Choose **Menu | Add | Text**. Press the **Tab** key to work in **Edit Mode**, and change the default text for the name of the game. In our case, we will use SAVE THE WHALE as the title.

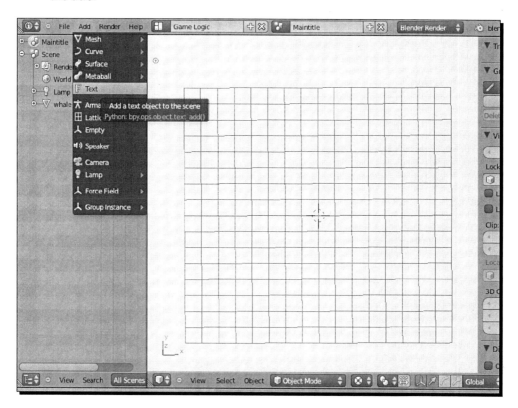

**3.** Press the **Tab** key to return to **Object Mode**, and add another text as shown in the following screenshot:

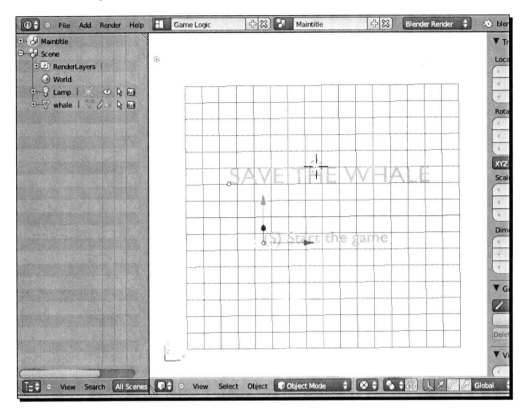

**4.** Go to the **Properties** interface. Select the **Text** tab and increase the **Extrude** option by 0.1 in the **Geometry** section, as shown in the next image. Extrude the text if you want volume in the titles:

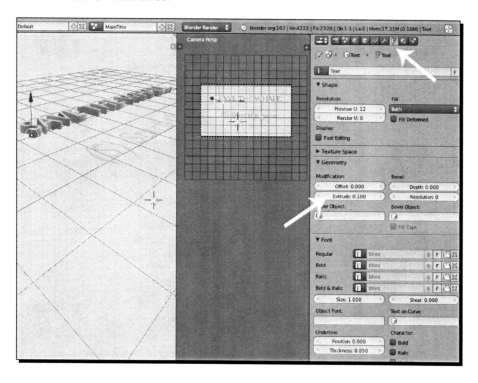

**5.** Choose **Menu | Add | Camera** for the top view. Split the 3D view in two areas and extend the camera as far as you wish. Move the camera enough to read all of the text. While moving the camera on the z axis and in one area, you will see the results on the second one. Press the *0* key to see through the camera.

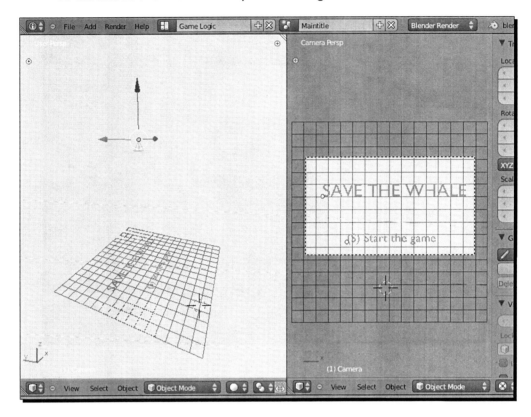

 Remember to have **Perspective View** in the left area to see the axis camera, and **Top View** in the right area to look inside it.

**6.** Press **Add | Mesh | Plane** with a color, and press **Add | Lamp | Spot** to add light. Press *F12* to see the rendered results, as shown in the following screenshot:

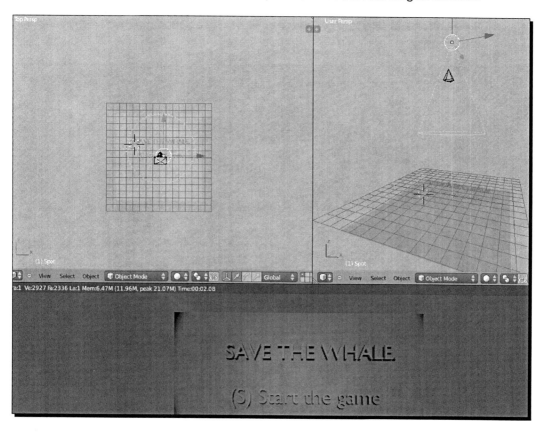

7. If you want to change the inside background of the plane, you can load an image of a background. In our case, we render (*F12*) a simple scene of *Chapter 4, Collisions*. Select the **Texture** tab in the **Properties** editor, and choose **New Texture** by pressing the + button and selecting the **Image** or **Movie type** option (no matter which image you choose ):

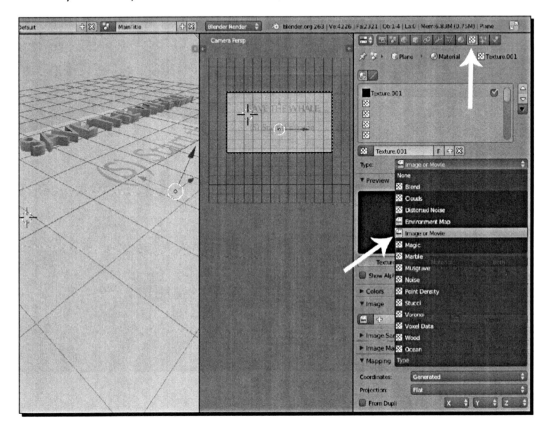

**8.** Press the **Open** button in the **Image** section, and select a photo of your folder. You can see the difference, but it's just a suggestion:

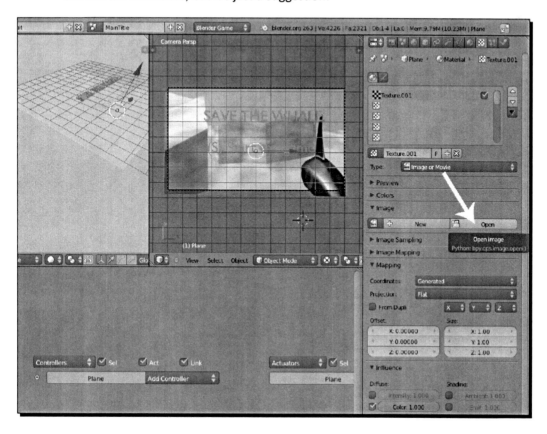

**9.** Delete the image of the plane for a better comprehension, select the second text, go to **Logic Editor**, and create **Keyboard** as the **Sensor**. Add **And** as the value for **Controller,** and choose **Scene** as the value for **Actuator**. Connect them as shown in the next image after pressing the *S* key in the box of the **Keyboard** sensor, and set **Scene** as level1 in the **Actuator** brick options.

 Remember, you must first create a new scene called level1.

## What just happened?

Really easy, right? We wanted to make our first splash screen and we have succeeded in doing so with just a few steps. We now have an impressive title and an option to choose from, which is to start playing. We have inserted the text, and using the logic bricks, we have connected the option (pressing the *S* key), to start playing the game to the scene of level 1.

## Have a go hero – game over

We have made the text of the introduction of the game. Why not try to make the final, which would be the end screen of the game. There is an actuator called **Game** that lets you exit the game, or also restart the game. Decide the best option you want for your first demo.

# Creating simple buttons

You can also make a dynamic home screen button and create a selection, that is, to choose the option you want, as you need to proceed further.

## Time for action – using the up or down options

If you only want to play with the up and down options to better visualize your choice, you can resort to the creation of a single button that complies with this specification. The most logical option is to create a button that has the capacity to move. Let's see it.

1. Use the text that we created in the previous example and add one more line of text, write the letter Q and the text Quit too:

 A plane has a short distance from all of the text.

2. Make a cube, scale it and put it in the middle of the text, and then place it, as shown in the following image:

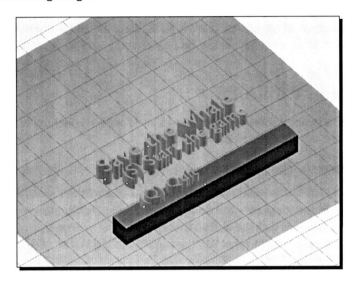

3. Make an animation. For example, in frame 1, the rectangle is above the first text, and in frame 2, it is above the second. Press *I* to insert a keyframe twice:

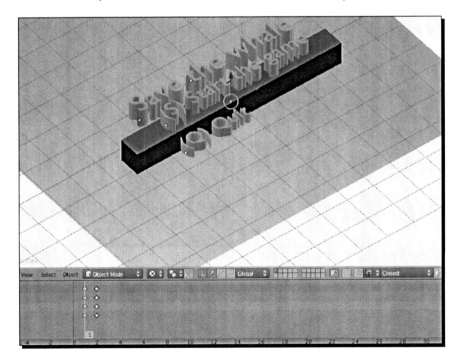

**4.** Select the rectangle, and go to **Logic Editor**. Add two **Sensors** called **Keyboard**, two **Controllers** called **And**, and two **Actuators** called **Action**. In the first **Keyboard** sensor, press the up arrow key, connect it with one controller, and finally with an **Action** actuator.

**5.** Indicating a **Play** type, select the action name for the rectangle, start from the left with frame 1 and select End frame with 1. Do the same with the second logic brick, as shown in the following image:

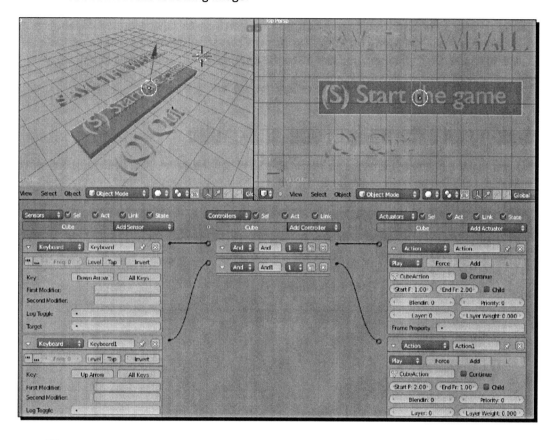

 Up or down **Keyboard** sensors have a different **Actions** actuator. Frame 1 is for the up arrow key, and frame 2 is for the down arrow key.

## *What just happened?*

We decided to place a moving object in the **Main** menu to have it set in the specific frame location that we have. By performing this simple action, we have entered enough information in the logic bricks to connect the up arrow or down arrow key with the position in the timeline of frame 1 or 2, whatever we decide.

## Have a go hero – creating transparent buttons

Can you create 50 percent transparent buttons? You can have this incorporated depending on where you are in the **Menu** options. Selecting the text should make the **Menu** option look lighter in shade. Or, if you dare, you can place the options that are not in use in Italics.

You can choose between these menu selection options to begin with.

# Making an externally executable game

Blender has the ability to generate an executable to install the game. But, by default, it is not activated. Let's see how we can awaken the beast.

## Time for action – exporting your game

It's time to export our game.

**1.** Go to **Menu | File | User Preferences**:

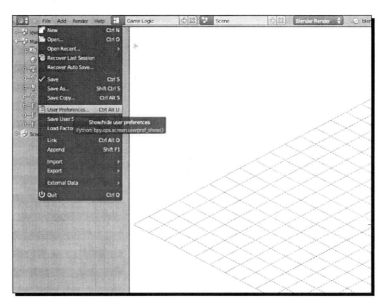

**2.** Choose **Addons**, and then select **Game Engine** in the left button panel, as shown in the following image. Check the box to say ok and close the panel.

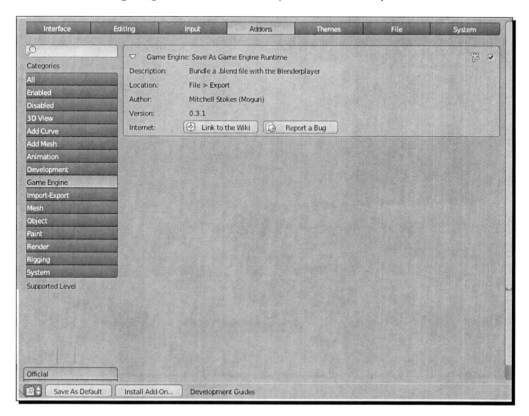

 You can click on the **Save As Default** button at the bottom of the screen if you don't wish to repeat the operation.

**3.** Choose **File | Export | Save As Game Engine Runtime** to get the executable:

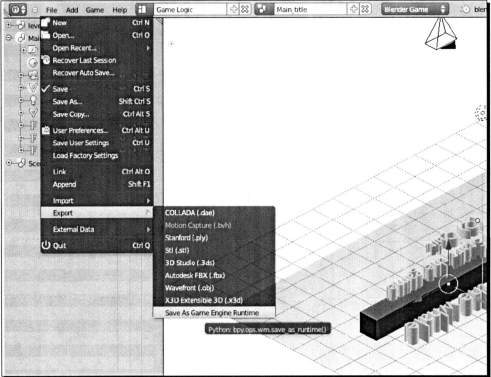

To include the music and textures, you must pack them in the .blend file before exporting. Choose **File | External Data | Pack** into the .blend file.

## *What just happened?*

We want to try and make a game engine executable render, so we must enable the **Game Engine Addon**, and export the file as **Game Engine Runtime**.

## Have a go hero – multiplayer game

The Internet is a library of tests to see what else you can apply to add on to Blender. Trying to get multi-player mode? You will see that with a little reinforcement, you can add this option in your game. When your friends try your online game, you really know you will be the hero for them.

## Pop quiz – making an external executable game

1. If you want to create a tittle, which option needs to be clicked in the 3D view?

    a. Main Scene

    b. New Scene

    c. New Layer

2. What kind of object needs to have a good start up fun if you have a background?

    a. Image

    b. Texture

    c. Sound

3. Which type of Actuator is needed in the logic brick to restart the player?

    a. Restart Game

    b. Restart Scene

    c. Pressing the Esc Key

# Summary

Well, this was a very important part of any game. There are people who specialize only in creating the covers of video games. We call them interface designers.

Good presentation with an understandable game menu is quite reasonable, right? There still are people who are not serious about the screens of game menus. If the first thing that you see when you play a game is not nice, will it not be disappointing? Bad impressions are difficult to overcome. Do not let go, but devote the necessary time to create the menus.

If you know that the front covers and back covers are as important as the game, then do not miss the last chapter of this book on how to promote your game. This is where you will expose your work and become famous.

# 8
# Publishing Your Game

*Now that you have the first version of your game made in Blender, it's time to bring it out and see what answers your creations have. It is very important to capture all of the positive and negative feedback without greatly affecting your way to make games. You will lose something when you start to change your idea of the game, if you take the comments of the people seriously. Sharpen your common sense to make your own contributions to create interesting and good things for your own game, and stop to remember those who do not provide good upgrades or are simply destructive. Do not get distracted in trying to justify any comments you have received. If you want to reach the public, the public also has the right to come to you.*

In this chapter, we will prepare the devices you have at hand, and exploit your initial project with simple challenges through the following topics:

◆ Uploading your game on the Web

◆ Making some trailers

◆ Creating something more

So let's get started.

## Playing your game on the Web

In the previous chapter, we learned to create a bootable game, but we may not have followers if the users are wary of simply clicking on an `.exe` file. The best way to combat this, and to avoid this risk, is to play the game directly on the Web, thanks to plug-in Burster. The **Burster** is an open source plug-in, which is free, and its source code is covered by the GPL license. If you need to learn about this plug-in, please `http:// visit www.geta3d.com`.

## Time for action – using the Burster plug-in

The Burster plug-in is especially dedicated to Blender users. All that you need to start with Burster is a web page. New users will be prompted by the web browser to download the Burster plug-in. To do that, let's embed the Burster player on the website. You need to insert the `<embed>` and `<object>` tags with a specified source file, width, and height of the player area. That's all. More information on using this browser's plug-in can be found on their website.

1. Upload the `.blend` file onto your web server and add the following code into your HTML file:

```
<OBJECT classid="CLSID:8318DE8B-B213-426b-B1B6-0A2589859898"
width="800"
height="600">
<PARAM name="type" value="application/x-burster"/>
<PARAM name="src" value="yourfile.blend" />
<embed type="application/x-burster"
src = "yourfile.blend"
width = "800"
hcight = "600">
</embed>
</OBJECT>
```

2. Upload your HTML file and make sure your `.blend` file has the file name you want to display at the page. A load bar shows you the progress of the `.blend` file upload on the Web:

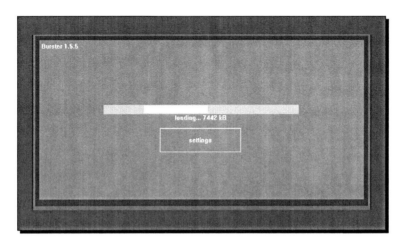

**3.** If everything is right, you will see something similar to the following image before you can play it in a browser:

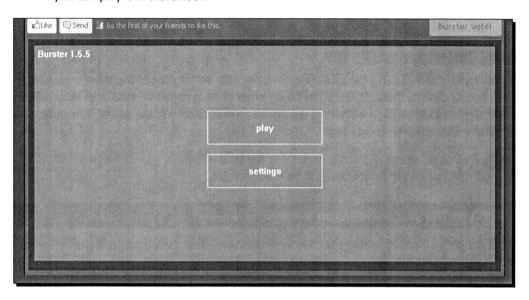

**4.** Press the **play** button to start the Blender game online. Your game should appear, as in the following screenshot:

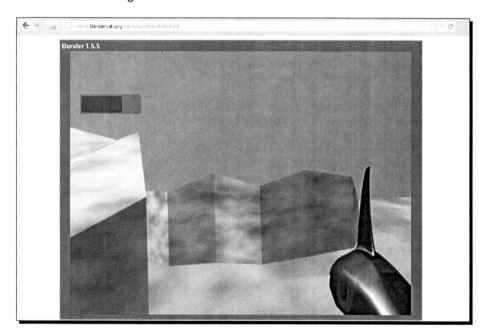

Click on **The Burster menu** tab to see some examples.

# What just happened?

We can upload the `.blend` file on the server using FTP, and thanks to the Burster plug-in, it can be run directly like a `.flash` file. All we need to do is copy the code, and change the name of `yourfile.blend` with what we have as the file name of our game. This code needs to go between the `body` tags.

Finally, we uploaded our HTML file. The HTML file (editable from a `.txt` file) and the `.blend` must be on the server, and will be ready for use.

## Have a go hero – customizing it

There are possibilities of setting the custom plug-ins' window colors. Just add the following code to your HTML file:

```
<OBJECT classid="CLSID:8318DE8B-B213-426b-B1B6-0A2589859898"

width="400"
height="300"

codebase="http://geta3d.com/geta3d/install/setup.msi">
<PARAM name="type" value="application/x-burster"/>

<PARAM name="src" value="yourfile.blend"/>
<PARAM name="pluginbg" value="#FF2233"/>

<PARAM name="progressbg" value="#4455EF"/>
<PARAM name="progressfill" value="#FBFF00"/>

<embed type="application/x-burster"
pluginspage="http://geta3d.com/"

src="/yourfile.blend"
width="400"

height="300"
pluginbg="#FF2233"

progressbg="#4455EF"
progressfill="#FBFF00">
</embed>
</OBJECT>
```

The color values are in hexadecimal `#BBGGRR` format. Let's see the parameters:

- `Plugin bg`: This sets the color of the plug-in's background window (default value: `#676767`)

- `progress bg`: This sets the color of the plug-in's progress bar background (default value: `#ABABAB`)

- `progress fill`: This sets the color of the plug-in's progress bar filling (default value: `#FCF7F7`)

- `codebase, pluginspage`: This specifies the address where the browser can find the plug-in and install it

If you don't want to use a `.txt` file or generate an HTML file, then you can upload to the server of the Burster web. Follow the instructions in their website, seen below:

# Making some trailers

Any game has a demo, but long before that, there is a preview of what this game is really like. The trailer is what sells and what attracts. If you make a good teaser to try your game, you will be successful. Let's see a brief trailer.

## Time for action – recording it

**CamStudio** is a utility for Windows that allows you to record everything that happens on your desktop, recording both the full screen, such as windows, and user defined areas. If you need to know more about this free program, please visit `http:// www.camstudio. org` or visit `http://en.wikibooks.org/wiki/Using_CamStudio`.

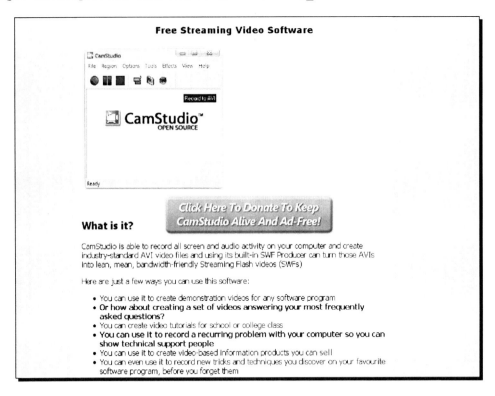

The following steps will enable us to record using CamStudio:

1.  Record three minutes of your game when you're playing it. Edit the three-minute video game and convert it into a one-minute exciting trailer.

**2.** Upload the video clip on your site announcing the game. You can see an example of the **RIO RAID** game in the following screenshot:

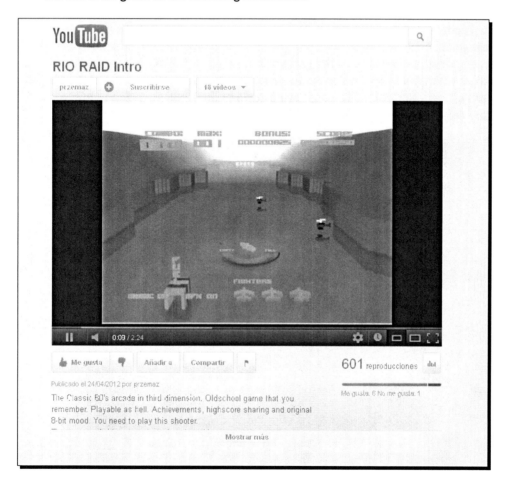

 See the response in the post shown in the YouTube channel, video, and so on.

## What just happened?

A trailer is a small excerpt from the video game to sell the game to a potential player. We recorded the minutes of starting an example, so that the users can see the style of the game. It shows an exact replica of the brief moments that your game has to offer. By recording your screen and editing the clips, you can create a fascinating trailer! Remember, a trailer of the release can increase your visits on the Web!

## Have a go hero – more records

The trailers are great since you can get a clear idea of what the game will be. If you want to create expectations, then do not stand halfway, and try to climb at least two trailers of your game: one that shows the same gameplay, and one that can be seen in detail in the the options and menus that the game offers. Do you think that there are players out there who would be interested in the making of the game? Do not reject the idea of explaining how you did it. Following is an example of the Sintel game (you can see it on `http://sintelgame.com/`):

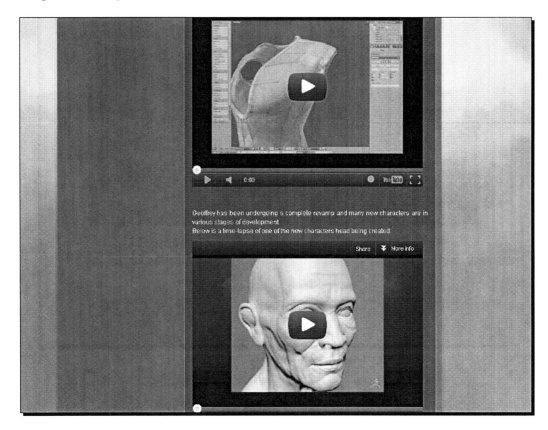

# Creating something more

There will always be the first version and the subsequent effort, if you really put it. Therefore, it is very important not to discard the games if you have one and only one version. To modify it, fix it, or simply tweak any of the choices to represent an improvement for the game. The version number of the game must be increased. Who wants to stay with Version 1 if you can get Version 3 or Version 4?

Only by insisting on changing the version will the product or game become new, perhaps a game that wants be something serious and insistent, that is there, constantly being updated to provide a better and improved product. This says a lot about yourself and your own game.

## Time for action – updating your game

A simple list of actions can make you see how updating the game enables you to finish it, and how close you are to making it.

*1.* Make some more menus as preferences or credits. See examples of the RAID Game shown before in the YouTube channel, and how get more information in their website, `http://rioraid.com/`.

The following image has more information than the preceding one:

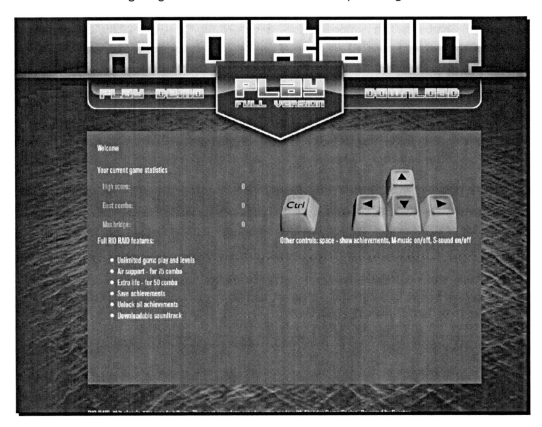

2. Change the textures of the game, by perhaps increasing the beauty of the first impression. This can be done by providing an example (extract to an example of the Burster web) with a screenshot of the game and their trailer. A good-looking Shooter game is made with Blender. See this personal Web at `http://vimeo.com/ gamerfreaq/`.

3. Make the character with three lives, make the big enemy with two lives, and the player greeting you. You can see an example of the Sintel game and how to improve it:

4. Search for bugs with tester players. They are very important to keep the game alive. If you face problems in resolving any question, you can follow this URL and read the forum related to the questions and support of BGEL: `http://www.blenderartists.org/forum/`.

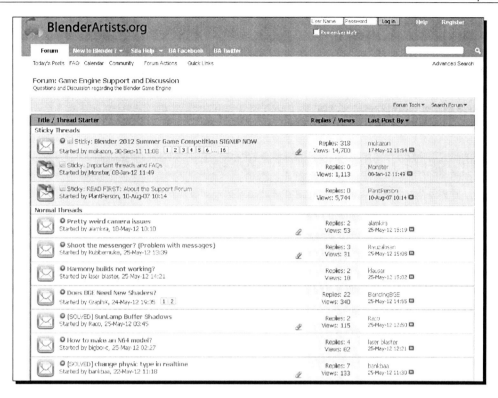

# *What just happened?*

We want the game to have more than one year, and we must therefore update it regularly. Upgrades to the higher versions should not be a mere arrangement of what did not work. We must also provide substance improvements that were not in the previous version. Our main objective must be to surprise the user, offering him an attractive game.

Adding more information on menus is welcome. Improving the look of the game worked by adding more textures, which made you see the game differently. Most remarkably, stress causes the enemy to resist the increase in difficulty in the game and eliminate the embarrassing mistakes. This will make certain that the game has a good reputation.

## Have a go hero – creating a new level 2

If you are really close to the first level, then without blowouts you can try a second level. The difficulty of the first level that you served is to minimize the work of the second. Many character's actions will not need to return to build it, and practically will no longer touch the interface of the game that cost you so much to organize. Just do the map and go to work. A new level awaits you!

## Pop quiz – creating something more

1. If you want to promote your game, what you will do?

   a. Show the game only to friends

   b. Try to sell the game

   c. Show the game on the website

2. Which kind of videos you need to make public?

   a. A game teaser

   b. A make of the game

   c. A teaser and its making

3. Which type of actions need to do something more about you game?

   a. Making a second level

   b. Starting with another first level game

   c. Improvement of the first level with sequels

# Summary

That's it, you may be thinking that this chapter has not been illustrative enough, but you need to reread the website again and again, since sometimes the most obvious is forgotten. If you follow these steps, your game will be talking about you and your game. Therefore, it is important to comment as many times as you have played your game.

In this chapter, we've already given enough clues. We covered how to create the content about your game through different ways of hanging it on the network, and other users to test and talk about it. As you will see, this is not the end of a book or your game. Just now, at this point, when your project is ready, is when it really starts to grow. Every action you take, has an impact in changing what you have, and this will be your routine until you decide yourself what to do with it.

I hope your project lasts long enough to feed you, and make you grow as you've built your own game. Do you remember your whole project before you started with this book? Well, now that change is not comparable with what lies ahead, the expectations are higher. You will have more difficult challenges in the project, much bigger than you could imagine.

So, happy blending!

# Pop Quiz Answers

The answers to the pop quizzes from each chapter are provided here for your reference. How did you score?

## Chapter 1, Things You Need to Know

### Pop quiz – exploring the interface of the Logic Editor

| 1 | a |
|---|---|
| 2 | b |
| 3 | d |

## Chapter 2, Your Characters

### Pop quiz – importing other files into Blender

| 1 | b |
|---|---|
| 2 | c |
| 3 | b |

## Pop quiz – involving enemies in the game

| 1 | b |
|---|---|
| 2 | c |
| 3 | c |

## Pop quiz – creating a meeting point

| 1 | c |
|---|---|
| 2 | b |
| 3 | a |

# Chapter 3, The First Level

## Pop quiz – blocking out a level environment

| 1 | b |
|---|---|
| 2 | a |
| 3 | b |

# Chapter 4, Collisions

## Pop quiz – respawning the character

| 1 | b |
|---|---|
| 2 | a |
| 3 | b |

# Chapter 5, Gameplay

## Pop quiz – moving to another level

| 1 | c |
|---|---|
| 2 | a |
| 3 | c |

# Chapter 6, Liven up Your World!

## Pop quiz – make your own game

| 1 | b |
|---|---|
| 2 | b |
| 3 | a |

# Chapter 7, Game Menu Screens

## Pop quiz – making an external executable game

| 1 | b |
|---|---|
| 2 | c |
| 3 | b |

# Chapter 8, Publishing Your Game

## Pop quiz – creating something more

| 1 | c |
|---|---|
| 2 | c |
| 3 | c |

# Index

## Thank you for buying
# Blender Game Engine Beginner's Guide

## About Packt Publishing

Packt, pronounced 'packed', published its first book "*Mastering phpMyAdmin for Effective MySQL Management*" in April 2004 and subsequently continued to specialize in publishing highly focused books on specific technologies and solutions.

Our books and publications share the experiences of your fellow IT professionals in adapting and customizing today's systems, applications, and frameworks. Our solution based books give you the knowledge and power to customize the software and technologies you're using to get the job done. Packt books are more specific and less general than the IT books you have seen in the past. Our unique business model allows us to bring you more focused information, giving you more of what you need to know, and less of what you don't.

Packt is a modern, yet unique publishing company, which focuses on producing quality, cutting-edge books for communities of developers, administrators, and newbies alike. For more information, please visit our website: www.packtpub.com.

## About Packt Open Source

In 2010, Packt launched two new brands, Packt Open Source and Packt Enterprise, in order to continue its focus on specialization. This book is part of the Packt Open Source brand, home to books published on software built around Open Source licences, and offering information to anybody from advanced developers to budding web designers. The Open Source brand also runs Packt's Open Source Royalty Scheme, by which Packt gives a royalty to each Open Source project about whose software a book is sold.

## Writing for Packt

We welcome all inquiries from people who are interested in authoring. Book proposals should be sent to author@packtpub.com. If your book idea is still at an early stage and you would like to discuss it first before writing a formal book proposal, contact us; one of our commissioning editors will get in touch with you.

We're not just looking for published authors; if you have strong technical skills but no writing experience, our experienced editors can help you develop a writing career, or simply get some additional reward for your expertise.

## Blender 3D Basics

ISBN: 978-1-849516-90-7    Paperback: 468 pages

The complete novice's guide to 3D modeling and animation

1. The best starter guide for complete newcomers to 3D modeling and animation

2. Easier learning curve than any other book on Blender

3. You will learn all the important foundation skills ready to apply to any 3D software

## Blender 2.5 HOTSHOT

ISBN: 978-1-849513-10-4    Paperback: 332 pages

Challenging and fun projects that will push your Blender skills to the limit

1. Exciting projects covering many areas: modeling, shading, lighting, compositing, animation, and the game engine

2. Strong emphasis on techniques and methodology for the best approach to each project

3. Utilization of many of the tools available in Blender 3D for developing moderately complex projects

4. Clear and concise explanations of working in 3D, along with insights into some important technical features of Blender 3D

Please check **www.PacktPub.com** for information on our titles

## Blender 2.5 Materials and Textures Cookbook

ISBN: 978-1-849512-88-6        Paperback: 312 pages

Over 80 great recipes to create life-like Blender objects

1. Master techniques to create believable natural surface materials

2. Take your models to the next level of realism or artistic development by using the material and texture settings within Blender 2.5.

3. Take the hassle out of material simulation by applying faster and more efficient material and texture strategies

## Google SketchUp for Game Design: Beginner's Guide

ISBN: 978-1-849691-34-5        Paperback: 270 pages

Create 3D game worlds complete with textures, levels, and props

1. Learn how to create realistic game worlds with Google's easy 3D modeling tool

2. Populate your games with realistic terrain, buildings, vehicles and objects

3. Import to game engines such as Unity 3D and create a first person 3D game simulation

4. Learn the skills you need to sell low polygon 3D objects in game asset stores

Please check **www.PacktPub.com** for information on our titles

Lightning Source UK Ltd.
Milton Keynes UK
UKOW011501230513

211099UK00002B/33/P